TUDOR
MONASTERY FARM

TUDOR
MONASTERY FARM

Life in rural England 500 years ago

BBC
BOOKS

Contents

INTRODUCTION

TOM

ayleaf Farmstead is in a beautiful part of West Sussex, surrounded by a mixture of green fields and woodland. There is an openness to it; it is never so hilly that you lose the horizon, yet its woods and forests provide an air of mystery.

Entering into our new guises as Tudor farmers, there was a blend of excitement and trepidation on our first day. What were we letting ourselves in for? As it turned out, life on the farm was to be a strange mix of sweat, blood and laughter. Hard work every day meant that we did perspire a lot – I don't think our period clothes will ever recover! I also bled weekly and picked up an array of interesting bruises that only became apparent when the adrenalin had worn off and the dirt had been removed. Most importantly, though, we laughed a lot. With Peter and Ruth there was always something to enjoy, and when things went wrong, there wasn't much else to do but throw up your hands and smile.

Almost as soon as we arrived, we saw that our commercial enterprises would have to take full advantage of our new environment. This included livestock, an arable crop and whatever raw materials we could source locally to aid our cause. The woods around our farmstead had many different species of tree, which would prove invaluable for making structures and tools. There were enough fields around that we could care for our livestock and grow our crop, all within a walk of the farmstead!

The weeks to come would be packed with everything from grappling with geese to constructing a pigsty, learning archery and blacksmithing, all rounded off with a hearty Tudor meal at the end of a long working day. We found that there's no other way to do a project like this other than to just roll up your sleeves, get involved and give everything a go.

In the course of the months that followed, we found some strategies helped us get accustomed to Tudor life. Our three top tips for survival were as follows:

ONE: EXPECT THE UNEXPECTED

There is no such thing as a five-minute job on a farm. Every day we had an idea of what we wanted to achieve throughout our working hours, breaking the day down into morning, afternoon and evening tasks. But on a Tudor farm, plans are a nice idea at best. Two hours' work with the cows could easily become four with very little to show for it. Inexplicably, the amount of coppice required was always more than our most prudent calculations had worked out.

We tried to keep our goals as realistic, achievable and time-orientated as possible and with time and experience we began to get a sense of how long each task would take – knowledge which in Tudor times would have been passed on from generation to generation, but which we were improvising for ourselves. (I say 'we' began to get a sense: Peter still believes there is such a thing as a five-minute job, even though to this day, he has never completed a job in five minutes or under. But still, you definitely can't fault his optimism!)

TWO: PUT IN 100% EVERY DAY

Never has the expression 'there are not enough hours in the day' seemed so relevant as they did on our farm. Not even with early starts and late finishes did we ever feel that we were on top. As a team it was crucial to keep pushing because, as it would have been in Tudor times, survival was a team effort.

A lot of Ruth's tasks, particularly around the house, were made harder because they were solo efforts. While Peter and I might have been involved in some big projects, we always had the luck, and sometimes joy, of being able to fall back on (or blame) someone else if things weren't going to plan. Of course, we all know that beer tastes best after a hard day's work, but on the Tudor farm that really was the light at the end of the farming tunnel.

" AS IT WOULD HAVE BEEN IN TUDOR TIMES, SURVIVAL WAS A TEAM EFFORT "

THREE: HAVE A SENSE OF HUMOUR

A high-pressure environment can often lead to mistakes and to stress. For Tudor farmers, their work was their livelihood; if a project failed, it could mean a hard year not just for them, but their family. It was a serious business, but laughter was a constant way of dealing with problems and easing some of the pressure. It allowed us to take a step back and look at why something was not working – why, for example, the geese refused to do as we wanted and then bit us for our trouble… We had to learn to take our situation seriously but also that to get through it, we had to lift ourselves. Laughter, not ale, was the answer.

A project like this can never fully recreate what the Tudors lived through but, we hoped, it would help us understand some of the hardships they faced, and to appreciate the difficulty of everyday life back at the start of the 16th century. At a time when so much could go wrong, our Tudor ancestors kept moving forward regardless, forging the way for new traditions and new technologies, some of which we still have today. All that remained was to see whether we could do the same…

MEET THE LAY FOLK

RUTH GOODMAN

I have to admit, I have always had a soft spot for the
Tudor era. So when the chance came up to explore
the early years, it was one that filled me with glee.
Whilst the Second World War is still, just, within living
memory, and the lifestyle of the Edwardian or even
Victorian farmer is only just out of our reach, the life,
thoughts and troubles of people who lived in 1500 are
truly remote from us. It requires a leap of imagination
to see yourself dressed all in wool brewing ale in a
huge copper pan, beating the laundry in the stream or
hauling your barley crop through the monastery gates.

Putting yourself in their shoes means embracing a
whole different way of thinking about the world. It was
a world with very little science but a great deal of faith:
one in which a woman's hair is a private, sexualised
part of the body to be seen only by her husband and
where a man's clothes reveal the shape of his legs; a
world that values spiritual above physical health, at a
time dogged by the horrors of the Black Death, the
sweating sickness and periods of real hunger.

Venturing into the late 15th and early 16th century promised to be a voyage
into a fascinatingly different life, but also one which still echoes down the
years. As we moved through the daily routine, little flashes of familiarity
kept popping up. Talk about 'drying up a cold' and you are calling on Tudor
medical advice, keeping your knife out of your mouth when eating is a way
to follow Tudor etiquette and porridge is a popular Tudor dish.

**❝ AS WE MOVED THROUGH THE DAILY
ROUTINE, LITTLE FLASHES OF
FAMILIARITY KEPT POPPING UP ❞**

It's a technologically exciting moment in time, too, from the arrival of printing to the development of the blast furnace for producing better, cheaper iron. Trade is beginning to expand as merchants bring new ideas about banking and finance from Italy into their daily practice and as the technology of shipping steps up.

Perhaps most importantly of all, the disease tide is turning. From 1348 onwards, epidemic after epidemic had driven down the population of Britain from nearly seven million people to less than two and a half million. But as the Tudor era began, the Black Death and the sweating sickness began to loosen their stranglehold and the nation started their march towards a globally influential role. The year 1500 is a moment when as a people we seem to take a deep breath, gather our strength and prepare for the future.

Perhaps, then, you can see why I was so delighted to have this opportunity to delve into the realities and practicalities of Tudor life: to sleep on straw, to hand milk sheep, to boil my own salt and to wear a veil. And the experience hasn't disappointed. I have had the chance to explore so many little niggling questions that have always bugged me and there have been so many revelations and 'Oh, I see' moments along the way. My brewing skills have leapt ahead. I have learned to garden with weeds (and enjoy eating them). I have been deafened by water-powered fulling mills and enchanted by sheep-grazed meadows.

I would not want to move there permanently but a prolonged visit to Britain in 1500 has been wonderful, exciting, enlightening and enormous fun.

PETER GINN

If I were actually living in Tudor times, by now I should probably be dead, or at the very least missing a couple of limbs. To work on a daily basis doing some of the jobs I have experienced as part of the Tudor Abbey Farm series, rather than just as a one-off, my life expectancy meter would be pointing to borrowed time.

> " IF I WERE ACTUALLY LIVING IN TUDOR TIMES, BY NOW I SHOULD PROBABLY BE DEAD, OR AT THE VERY LEAST MISSING A COUPLE OF LIMBS "

It was with a sense of excitement and trepidation that I donned my doublet, hiked up my hose and stepped out into Tudor England during the reign of Henry VII. I always count myself as being very lucky when I get to participate in a project like this. It is a chance to get your hands dirty, to put on the clothes and do the work of our ancestors and find out just what life was like 500 years ago.

It was a time when England was only really emerging as a nation and had yet to form a union with Scotland. The Church was the principal landowner and farming was a slightly more rural affair. I was most looking forward to getting to grips with our cows, not as livestock to be reared as food or for milk, but as beasts of burden engaged on the land doing the heavy work.

Equally the fabrics that we encounter in life – the wood, the metals and the glass – were cutting edge technologies back then. It was the monasteries and entrepreneurial farmers who were early adopters and experimenters. I find that by following a material on its journey from its raw state to a finished product you can gain a better understanding of the impact it had on society: we certainly got a strong sense of that during our time on the farm.

Each time I embark upon one of our time-travelling adventures I am always reminded just how much work was involved in doing pretty much anything – shopping, cooking, even washing up. Sometimes we can forget how hard life can be and if we learned one lesson, it was the fact that someone, somewhere has to do the hard work. In our modern lives we take so many things for granted that this trip back in time was a real reminder of the hard work and ingenuity of the Tudors that we still reap the benefits of today.

TOM PINFOLD

The Tudor period saw unbelievable changes in the political and religious fabric of England. In 1485, the Church was a constant that royal houses could only aspire to; to work as a tenant farmer on a monastic farm was to understand the whole ecosystem that one exists within.

The influences on farm life were varied but the tenant farmer on monastic land had to learn to work in subservient partnership with the monks, knowing that however hard they worked a percentage of what they grew, earned and produced would go to the monastery. The price of failure, meanwhile, could be eviction.

As a military historian, farming is not necessarily something that comes naturally (though of course, military and social history are so closely interlinked, and none more so than the Tudor period). However, as someone who is also an archaeologist, the chance to

study history practically was an opportunity that does not come around regularly and was to be embraced.

Peter and Ruth are old hands at period farm life. I, on the other hand, am not and I would be lying if I said there was not some trepidation at the beginning and an uncertainty as to what I had got involved with. Reassuringly, though, the shine in Peter's eyes as

> **❝ THE SHINE IN PETER'S EYES AS THE FIRST DAY APPROACHED DISPLAYED MORE OF A BOYISH EXCITEMENT THAN A MANIACAL GLINT! ❞**

the first day approached displayed more of a boyish excitement than a maniacal glint! Working on a project like Tudor Abbey Farm can only be done if one is willing to get involved with every task and activity that comes along. The great thing about farm life in the Tudor period is the diverse range of activities one gets to experience from the more common skills like woodworking to the more wide-ranging jobs of blacksmithing or shepherding, even beekeeping.

Preparing for Tudor farm life is difficult. Fitness is subjective but one can never fully prepare for a job like this as the body will be challenged constantly. Reading books and archaeological reports can give a view of the Tudor period but it does not prepare one physically for what lies ahead. The daily grind of our Tudor farm, however, was only part of it. An important component of the experience was the costume. On cold days it could be very comfortable and surprisingly warm. On warm days it could be very uncomfortable and even warmer! Yet the more I wore it, the more attached I became to it. I realised how important a factor period dress was to the whole experience, the benefits and the downsides.

Completing a Tudor farm project means embracing every aspect of the farm: the physical, the emotional and the spiritual. The centrality of religion to the Tudor period means that you must work within the same constraints and guidelines, and that an appreciation of the religious influence on our daily life must be sought.

THE MONASTIC SYSTEM

Throughout the endless dynastic changeovers of the civil war years, the Church had remained a constant in the lives of lay folk working on farms, as it was for all English people at the time. Henry VII saw strong ties with the Church as the key to influencing people in their everyday lives, morally and politically.

In the aftermath of the Battle of Bosworth in 1485, King Henry's crown may not been have secure, but his influence on the monasteries seemed certain. None of them could have foreseen the political upheaval that was to take place in the years to come.

LIVING IN THE CHURCH

T he Tudor Age began with the monastic system firmly embedded in all aspects of English life: every county had at least one monastery, with 513 monasteries and 130 nunneries throughout England and Wales in total. The monasteries owned huge areas of land, with a wide variety of laymen working in, for and around them. They were focal points for trade, taking cuts of the profits and flourishing from the land they rented out to yeoman farmers. It was a symbiotic relationship between the monastery and the working man, with both requiring each other to prosper.

The physical space of the cloister stood as a symbol for the enclosed, contemplative life of the monasteries

When Henry VIII called for a full survey of all the religious houses prior to the dissolution of the monasteries, his officials recorded around 4,000 monks and 2,000 nuns. In addition there were something in the region of 3,000 regular canons and another 3,000 friars who worked among laypeople, rather than following the enclosed life. Despite being small in number, these few people and the institutions that they inhabited owned perhaps as much as a quarter of the landed wealth in England. According to the tax assessment of 1535 they received an annual income of £165,500, a sum close to twice the annual income of the King.

CHURCH DEPENDANTS

It is tempting to think that such small numbers in a population of around 2.8 million reflected a great falling-off in the monastic life of the country. This, though, is not so; there were never very many more people living under the monastic rule. The monasteries were not in serious decline but largely operating at full strength, with plenty of potential

As well as living a life of regulated communal prayer, monks also had to care for and supervise their large estates

recruits ready to join the religious life whenever there should be room for them. Supporting someone in a purely contemplative, non-productive life is expensive, and since it is a lifelong commitment the resources required are extensive. Medieval and early Tudor Britain could not comfortably provide this lifestyle for too many healthy active adults.

Though the number of actual monks and nuns was small, the number of people whose livelihoods were bound up with the monastic institutions was much larger. Lay workers and servants directly employed by the abbeys, priories and convents far outnumbered the religious inhabitants.

" AROUND 25,000 PEOPLE WERE DEPENDENT UPON THE MONASTERIES FOR THEIR DAILY BREAD AT ANY ONE TIME "

At wealthy abbeys, there was a ratio of 30 workers for every monk, although the majority of poorer institutions – particularly nunneries – rarely had a ratio of more than one to one. These workers were the people who baked the bread and brewed the ale, laundered the clothes and served the meals. They cared for the horses in the stables, took the grain to the miller, dug the gardens and swept the floors. Many wealthier monks and nuns even employed their own personal servants to look after them in a style similar to that in which they had grown up.

Monastic houses also served as home for a number of long-term guests and their servants. Most institutions housed a few people who had, in effect,

Our parish church was one of those where monks performed the duties of a parish priest

bought a pension: in exchange for a gift of money or land, these people secured a guarantee of a room and a daily food ration for life. Other guests came and went. Some just stayed the night as they journeyed across the country, others stayed for weeks or months to visit relatives within the monastery, or be near to family in the surrounding district. There were some who used the guesthouses as refuges from difficult situations at home or places to park relatives in safety until other arrangements (marriages for example) could be made. Most of the guests made some sort of financial contribution, although as surviving monastic account books make clear hospitality could be a major burden upon the order's finances.

> **❝ THE REGULAR ROUND OF PRAYER WAS EXPECTED NOT ONLY TO AID THE SOULS OF THE MONKS AND NUNS BUT ALSO ANYONE WHO SUPPORTED THEM PRACTICALLY OR FINANCIALLY ❞**

In total, around 25,000 people were dependent upon the monasteries for their daily bread at any one time. They all lived to a religious timetable, following, to one degree or another, the rules of the order.

RELIGIOUS LIFE

The main purpose of the religious life was prayer: communal, formal prayer to be supplemented by periods of private devotions. Monks and nuns would come together at fixed times to recite a given round of texts suited to the time of day and the religious calendar. Several different orders maintained monasteries in Britain, including the Benedictines, Cistercians, Augustinians, Gilbertines and Brigittines.

St Benedict's rule was perhaps the most influential, and most other houses followed a similar pattern. The religious day began according to his rule with Matins at midnight, followed by services 'at the first, third, sixth, ninth hours, at Vesper time and at Compline'. In between these formal services were periods of rest for sleep, food and exercise, and times for private prayer. Most religious orders required long periods of silence to facilitate contemplation. The regular round of prayer was expected not only to aid the souls of the monks and nuns but also anyone who supported them practically or financially in their endeavours. They prayed for the sake of all people as an act of charity and devotion. In between their religious duties, many monks and nuns also provided the managerial element of their foundation's needs: keeping accounts, supervising staff, and negotiating contracts for supplies or rental agreements. Around half of the resident religious had some sort of administrative role.

Guests and servants were not required to attend all the services but many chose to attend where it fitted into their daily routine, seeking the benefit to their souls of a proximity to and participation with the monastic round. Working within a monastery may well have been sought out as a position by poorer laypeople who felt a calling to the life of prayer, but whose social and financial position ruled out full membership of the community. The ranks of the cloister were rarely filled by members of the aristocracy, or even of the wealthiest gentry families, but equally they were not recruited from among the poor, the artisan or the labourer. Most monks and nuns had grown up in the families of the minor gentry and merchant classes, and while the orders vowed humility and poverty, life in the Church was certainly comfortable and, to Tudor minds at least, secure.

The regular repetition of formalised prayer formed the core purpose of monastic life

THE CHURCH AS LANDOWNER

Beyond the ranks of the cloister were large numbers of people for whom the monastery was the landlord. Before the Black Death arrived on these shores, the monasteries had held direct control of the farming of their lands. Monks had supervised staff in the day-to-day business of growing crops and raising sheep and had operated as vast agricultural businesses.

A chain of small daughter houses had provided accommodation to those who needed to be based far from the main monastery in order to carry out this supervisory and managerial role. By taking advantage of economies of scale and being able to hire the most skilled workers, the monasteries had been able to generate much higher incomes from the land than the peasant farmers of surrounding areas. All that, though, began to change after 1348.

THE BLACK DEATH

When the plague struck and killed around one third of the population, the economic balance shifted. People who survived discovered that a shortage of labour offered new opportunities to those at the bottom of the pile. With fewer mouths to feed, there was less demand for grain and prices fell. Wages began to creep slowly upwards, and it became harder for landowners to enforce their rights over those who had been hitherto bound to the land by law.

The nation's recovery from the Black Death was slow. Wave after wave of plague continued to hit and soon the increasingly virulent 'sweating sickness' began to rival the bubonic plague in the death toll. In 1348 the population of England had stood at around 6.4 million; by 1400 it was hovering at around 4 million and over the next century it continued to slowly fall. By 1500 there were around 2.8 million people in England – almost exactly the same number that there had been in 1086, when the Domesday Book was compiled.

The Black Death was no respecter of class or lifestyle, and monks suffered alongside lay folk

This was the economic reality that monasteries had to cope with: a small population, falling grain prices, low levels of profit from arable land, and a workforce that could now up and leave if it wished to. In many areas of the country, monasteries had responded after the first crash in population by becoming sheep farming specialists. Unable to find cheap labour to plough and sow, they allowed land to revert to pasture. Farms without tenants were allowed to fall into disrepair, before finally being pulled down. All the while, large flocks became larger, tended by a few shepherds ranging over areas that had once been corn fields. The monasteries managed to survive, but at the cost of whole villages disappearing from the landscape.

By 1450 monks had largely stopped direct farming; now they rented out their lands to people like us

> **❝ THE MONASTERIES MANAGED TO SURVIVE, BUT AT THE COST OF WHOLE VILLAGES DISAPPEARING ❞**

A CHANGING MARKET

By 1450, monastic farming had shifted again. Other European regions had improved the quality and quantity of their sheep flocks, depressing the market for British fleeces and reducing the profits from the sale of raw wool. The nature of the wool trade had changed from the exporting of raw material to finished cloth instead, and monasteries were not well placed to make the same move. It was merchants who could invest in the manufacturing side of the business that were coming to the fore.

Agricultural profits, both arable and livestock, had become uncertain and unpredictable, and monks and nuns had to adjust their strategy. As major landowners they began to lease out their land for fixed rents to independent tenants. This shifted the risk away from them and onto the tenant farmers: once the agreement was signed, the monastery could be assured of a stable income whatever the weather or market forces brought. Monasteries no longer operated as powerful agri-businesses, but as great landowners with a diversified portfolio. Most monasteries held some land directly to grow food for the monks. Many continued to use hilly areas as sheep farming land and others maintained an interest in mining or the dues from parish churches. Rents from farmland, however, had become a crucial, possibly the major, source of their income.

*The marketplace: a focus for
the more ambitious members of
the agricultural community*

TENANT FARMING

It was as this new breed of tenant farmers that we were to enter the scene.
The monastery was our landlord: tying us to the economic life of the
monks. Monasteries generally preferred to rent out their farms to the more
prosperous and successful of the peasant farmers: those who would be able
to pay higher rents and who were less likely to fail. They often chose to offer
slightly larger blocks of land than that
which formed the usual peasant holding.
This was because it was much easier to
manage a small number of medium-to-large
sized units than a plethora of small blocks
of land.

> ❝ THE MONASTERY WAS
> OUR LANDLORD: TYING
> US TO THE ECONOMIC
> LIFE OF THE MONKS ❞

Wealthier farmers also brought more complete stocks of tools and farm
equipment with them, releasing an abbey from the need to provide such
things as part of the tenancy agreement. In return, these prosperous
farmers expected to rent better quality land and farm buildings in a good
state of repair. In the uncertain economic climate of the late 15th and early
16th century, the arrangement was a sensible one for the religious houses.

Our home was large and well maintained; a real 'des res'

As the economy began to pick up pace later in the century, it put those monastic tenant farmers in a very good position to make the most of the new opportunities. It was to be farmers like us who would rise to be the prosperous yeomen – the new middle classes – of the future.

PAYING THE RENT

Monastic rents could be paid in cash or kind, or very occasionally in labour. Although cash was increasingly popular with landlords, the monasteries retained some rents in kind, in particular malted barley (for the monks' ale) or wool to help make up the monasteries' own 'clip'. The quality of goods paid as rent in kind was naturally a matter of great concern to the monks and regular inspection visits and long discussions about farming practice was expected of a well-managed religious community. Monastic landlords could be quite 'hands on' with those farms that lay in close proximity to the community, keeping an eye on building repairs, fences, ditches and stocking levels to prevent long-term overgrazing.

On a purely practical and business footing, we were to have many dealings with the monks outside the religious and spiritual relationship. With such vast swathes of land being owned by the monastic houses, our experience of life as tenants to the monks was a common one. It was also an experience that reflected those whose landlord was a layperson. Monasteries as landlords appear in the records as neither particularly generous, nor particularly hard-hearted. They followed the society-wide patterns of land holding, attempting to maintain their income in fluctuating economic circumstances.

DAILY RATIONS

RUTH

Food and drink played a central role in the monastic life, and not just because they were large communities that needed to eat and organise their provisioning. The charitable giving of food formed a large part of their daily work and a carefully-controlled diet was also, in theory at least, part of their religious observance.

The monastic rule dictated the times of meals and the quantity and type of food and drink on offer, as well as outlining a calendar of feast and fast that formed the ritual year. Monks had dinner every day (a meal taken in the late morning, around 11 o'clock) but supper (served at around 6 o'clock) was only served from Easter until 13th September (and not on Wednesdays and Fridays). Dinner consisted of two cooked dishes alongside the daily ration of bread and ale (wine in the Mediterranean original) and the meat of four-footed animals was entirely prohibited. Supper was unspecified but seems to have been intended to be simply bread and ale.

THE BASICS

Bread and ale, then, were the most important foodstuffs, just as they were for the lay population. The rule in most foundations allotted one large loaf of bread and one gallon (or eight pints) of ale a day to each monk. The bread was pure wheat bread in most cases, although sometimes maslin (a mixture of approximately 80% wheat and 20% rye) appears in the record. The flour was sifted to remove most of the bran, yielding a fine, high quality white loaf that weighed around 2 lb: such a loaf has been calculated to provide 2,550 calories. The ale was also a superior product and was made from the first mash: this could have delivered another 1,280 calories. Together with the two cooked dishes a day at dinner, this was a very substantial amount of food, although concentrated for many days of the year into just one daily meal.

> " THIS WAS A VERY SUBSTANTIAL AMOUNT OF FOOD CONCENTRATED INTO ONE DAILY MEAL "

Monastic food was often simple but very plentiful

The portions of other foods served to the monks were also generous with, for example, about one and a half pounds of fish being allocated to each monk. This was divided between the two different dishes that the rule allowed. By contrast, a main course fish dish at most modern restaurants would usually weigh between a quarter and a third of a pound – a comparison which highlights the protein and calorie rich nature of the monastic diet.

FISH

Fish were synonymous with fast days and were eaten every Wednesday, Friday and Saturday as well as all of both Lent and Advent. In total, 215 days a year were fish days and no meat, including two-footed poultry, was permitted. The fish on offer was dominated by the cod family: cod itself, along with ling and haburden, was available fresh, salted and pickled. Herrings – fresh, salted and smoked – were also prominent items on the main menu.

" OFFCUTS NOW ENTERED THE ORDINARY DIET OF MONKS, WITH THE ARGUMENT THAT THEY DID NOT REALLY CONSTITUTE 'PROPER' MEAT "

Communal eating and dietary restrictions were an important element of religious life

SPECIAL PLEADINGS

By 1500, however, the actual diet of both monks and nuns had wandered somewhat from this standard. Those who still came closest to it were the inhabitants of the poorest houses, generally nuns, whose income permitted little else and who were most influenced by a culture that lauded female restraint, poverty and asceticism.

For the majority of early Tudor religious brethren, meat had crept in to the main diet (poultry had never been forbidden, except on fish days). A distinction was made between butcher's meat, which continued to be restricted, and all the other offcuts: offal, fat, gelatine and trimmings now entered the ordinary diet of monks, with the argument that they did not really constitute 'proper' meat. Meaty dishes as opposed to dishes of meat were happily served and consumed in the refectory.

A further refinement of the special pleading was made between pure slabs of meat and bits of meat that were simply one ingredient among several; a beef pottage that also contained beans and vegetables was acceptable in many religious houses, even if a joint of roast beef was not.

The dietary restrictions were circumvented still further in many monasteries by building a totally separate room for eating. St Benedict's instructions concerned only food that was eaten in the abbey's refectory. So, increasingly, monks would also dine in a separate room,

'Meaty' dishes, where meat was combined with other ingredients, had come to be seen as acceptable – they didn't count as 'meat'

generally called a misericord, which was taken to be outside the rule and not subject to its restrictions.

At Westminster Abbey, a Benedictine foundation, the monks appear to have operated a rota system: some ate in the refectory where meaty dishes could be served, whilst others enjoyed plain meat in the misericord (the exception was on fish or fasting days when everyone ate together in the refectory). The rota allowed everyone a chance to enjoy the richer diet whilst fulfilling (to the letter, if not the spirit, of the law) the injunction to eat together according to rule in the refectory. Misericords are to be found at most of the 800-plus monastic communities; kitchen accounts, where they survive, confirm that this was a widely established practice.

CIRCUMVENTING THE RULES

The meat served in the misericord consisted primarily of mutton and beef, with pork and veal not all that far behind: the offal and trimmings of cows, sheep and pigs would appear in the meaty dishes of the refectory on the same days. Portion sizes, again, were vast. In the refectory something in the region of three quarters of a pound of meat and offal was available in the two permitted dishes, while in the misericord it was around three times that amount.

Further variation came from the custom of 'pittances'. On special occasions, often associated with the multitude of saints days, an additional dish or pittance was granted to some or all of the brethren. Many benefactors seeking the prayers of the monks gave money specifically to this end. Pittances were treat foods: not the solid basics of the rule's two general dishes but game and freshwater fish such as partridges, woodcock, salmon or trout.

Dairy produce and eggs formed another significant element of the monastic diet. They were permitted on meat days and throughout Advent, but forbidden in Lent and on Fridays. Purchases of eggs and produce at Westminster indicate around five eggs per monk on every

Forbidden during Lent and fish days, eggs were enjoyed the rest of the year

day they were allowed, along with around half a pint of milk and plenty of butter for cooking with.

Away from the refectory and misericord, there were other opportunities for food. The sick had always been exempt from the rule and ate whatever the infirmarer considered suitable for their health in the infirmary. Many monks, busy with their administrative duties, were unable or unwilling to join their brethren in the refectory: they had their food sent up to their rooms or offices and whilst this could have simply consisted of the same dishes that everyone else was eating, it was often taken as an opportunity for more personal dietary control.

Senior officials were able to supplement or replace the usual fare with dishes either brought in from outside, purchased separately from the abbey cooks or cooked by their own servants specifically for them. Some non-office holding monks were also able to set up separate 'households' within the monastery, sharing semi-private rooms and employing their own servants to cook and care for them: once again circumventing many of the dietary rules and restrictions. Attendances at the refectory table could be well below half the total number of residents. Adherence to the cycle of meat and fish days, however, seems to have been universally observed. Monks may well have pushed at the boundaries of the rule in search of more interesting and fashionable foodstuffs but the idea of fasting in remembrance of the basic Christian cycle remained a powerful one. So much so, in fact, that many laypeople were just as meticulous on this score.

AN ABBOT'S DIET

Abbots enjoyed a diet and lifestyle that was quite distinct from their brothers. As leaders of the community, they were expected to live and entertain in a style that befitted someone of equal status in the lay world. For the largest and richest houses, this meant living on a par with a lord and even for the abbots of poorer institutions, a lifestyle comparable with the senior gentry of the area was kept up. Abbots had their own cooking arrangements and usually their own kitchens and staff to run them. They were required to follow the pattern of fast and feast, with fish and meat days, but there was no restriction upon quantity or quality.

> « MONKS AT THE TIME HAD A REPUTATION AS FAT MEN IN A WORLD OF THIN PEOPLE »

An abbot could invite selected members of his brethren to join him at table; the most successful and well-liked abbots made a point of spreading their favours among the whole community as an occasional treat and reward for good behaviour. When he had guests, the abbot used the opportunity afforded by generous hospitality to maintain and win the goodwill of powerful and influential laymen. Feasting the guests of the abbey also served to maintain the status of the institution in a world that associated hospitality and largesse with nobility and legitimate lordship. An abbot who maintained a poor table was one who would find endowments to the foundation few and far between, the status of his applicants dropping and his local influence restricted.

FEEDING THE POOR

With so much food on offer, it is perhaps no surprise that the skeletons of monks reveal patterns of disease associated with obesity – patterns markedly different from those found in the ordinary parish graveyard. Monks at the time had a reputation as fat men in a world of thin people. However, they did not eat all of the gargantuan portions of food that was put in front of them. Leftovers were part of the charitable giving of monasteries, part of the way in which they fed the poor.

" SOME OF THESE DOLES COULD BE ENORMOUS WITH SEVERAL HUNDRED PORTIONS DISTRIBUTED IN A SINGLE DAY "

Some food went directly to the poor, produced separately under the aegis of the almoner and distributed at the abbey gate on particular feast days. This tended to be in the form of coarser, non-wheat bread, pottages of peas and beans, and with the weakest sort of ale. Some of this provision was distributed on a daily basis, but many of the bequests that funded the activity required periodic large-scale handouts in celebration of particular saints days or in remembrance of the anniversary of the death of certain individuals. Some of these doles could be enormous, with several hundred portions distributed in a single day – taxing the organisational ability of the abbey as well as its finances. Other food came daily from the refectory table.

The huge portions allotted to the monks allowed for a regular surplus, the least appetising segment being that which was most likely to find its way to the abbey gate (though few poor people were going to turn their noses up at white wheaten bread and pottage with meat in it). The amount of food handed out was subject to variation. On days when the monks received a pittance in addition to their usual fare, the amount of leftovers naturally rose; on fasting supper-less days, particularly in Lent, the surplus could be quite small. The appetites of the religious inhabitants could be an important matter for those waiting hungrily outside.

Monastic leftovers formed one of the regular acts of charitable giving that the rule required

DAILY MENUS

MENUS FOR LENT

FOR AN ABBOT

Dinner
Conger eel in vinegar sauce, salmon baked in pastry, pike roasted, herring vaunts, roach in green sauce (a crushed herb mixture), a moyse (made with almond milk thickened with rice to a custard consistency, seasoned with sugar) white bread and wine.

Supper
A dish of whiting, baked eel, mortice of salmon (like a terrine), white bread and wine.

FOR A MONK

Dinner
White wheaten bread, boiled cod (fresh cod poached in milk), vaunts of red herring (smoked herring, oatmeal, minced onion and herbs made up into fishcakes), strong ale.

FOR A TENANT FARMER

Breakfast
Brown bread and ale.

Dinner
Brown bread, salt cod pottage with beans and cabbage and ale.

Supper
Brown bread and ale.

MENUS FOR A MEAT EATING DAY

FOR AN ABBOT
(ON A DAY WITHOUT ANY IMPORTANT GUESTS)

Dinner
Boiled beef, boiled mutton, roast pork, roast mutton, a couple of roasted conies (rabbits), a dish of woodcock, a custard, white bread and wine.

Supper
Vaunts of veal (small veal and dried fruit pies), an egg froyse, capons upon sops (boiled chicken with a sauce of chicken stock, spices and raisins served upon toasted bread), white bread and wine.

FOR A MONK

Dinner
Most of a large loaf of white, wheaten bread, beef pottage, a dish of froyse flesche (minced meat bound with egg and breadcrumbs, fried like beef burgers) and an egge froyse (a solid sort of omelette with breadcrumbs and sometimes a little bit of shredded bacon). Accompanied by strong ale.

Supper
The rest of the white bread and a neat's tongue served with a sauce with more ale to drink.

FOR A TENANT FARMER
(LIKE OURSELVES)

Breakfast
Brown bread (half wheat and half rye) and a drink of weak ale.

Dinner
Brown bread, beef pottage with plenty of beans and vegetables and ale to drink.

Supper
Brown bread, a piece of cheese and some more ale.

A DAY IN THE LIFE OF A MONK

TOM

Men and women could join a religious institution in England at any time in adulthood. However, it was widely believed that men had more free will in this decision than some of the women who became nuns – one observation was that nunneries became dumping grounds for unmarried daughters that parents were no longer prepared to support. This might seem harsh to 21st-century sensibilities but, as with any lifestyle, there were good and not-so-good points to monastic life: one of the pluses was that it did guarantee a form of security.

Our monastery administrator; here smiling, but that depended on our success as tenant farmers!

There were a variety of monastic orders one could join. Each one had their own individual anomalies but as a whole they followed the same daily structure. Three vows were typically observed – poverty, chastity and obedience – but monastic life itself was not always so clear cut. As financial centres the monasteries profited from trade and at the start of the Tudor period, the morality of the monks and nuns of many institutions had been called into question: some monks were accused of smuggling in women for their carnal pleasure and some abbesses of having children.

However, despite the acts of some, the monasteries remained for very practical reasons; they provided jobs for local people, they were places of hospitality for weary travellers and they were the religious focal points of their communities. In fact, the monks had become the minority in monasteries by the Tudor period, employing laymen, servants, agricultural workers and receiving visitors both secular and religious on a constant basis.

❝ MONASTIC LIFE WAS NOT EASY, BUT THEN IT WAS NEVER INTENDED TO BE ❞

Throughout the working day the monk had three main objectives: to pray, to work and to study. Of these the skeleton of the day and night was made up of prayer, roughly every three hours; work and study were thus the 'flesh' to these 'bones'. Prayer was for God, while work and study, though in honour of God, were also required to keep the institutions going. Monastic life was not easy, but then it was never intended to be. By making personal sacrifice the men and women who took the vows were proving their piety and obedience to God.

PRAYER

Prayers were the focus of a monk's day. These took place eight times a day in fact, and it was believed that this act of piety would secure the monk's salvation in the next life. The times were set out in the Book of Hours, the major prayer book, with each 'hour' representing a specific time when prayers should be read. The monk who took on the job of reading the lessons was called the Lector, with the times for prayer known as Matins, Lauds, Prime, Terce, Sext, Nones, Vespers and Compline. These times were set in stone: whenever it got to prayer time, all work ceased and the monks had to attend the relevant service. It was a constant cyclic process and together with religious festivals dictating the Tudor calendar, monks had a permanent routine on both the macro and the micro level.

WORK

The monks had various responsibilities within and for the monastery. They ran the monastery itself through a hierarchical structure, supervised the labourers and, as landlords, inspected the monastery's property and collected rent money from their tenants. The emphasis on a monk's life was simplicity, but due to the vast diversity of requirements within the monastery, he could find himself doing a variety of jobs throughout the week. On any given day a monk could be carrying out medical duties, dealing with the poor, stocktaking or monastery administration.

A miniature from the Book of Hours, showing tenant farmers harvesting their crops in June

" IN MOST OF THEIR BUSINESS TRANSACTIONS THE MONKS WERE THE DOMINANT PARTNER "

The monks took a direct interest in their tenant farmers and they were not above bringing in experts for certain dealings, emphasising the strong links the monks had with business. When assessing the quality of wool,

A day spent checking up on tenant farmers and deep in contemplation meant the physical and spiritual requirements of a monk were met

for example, an expert could be brought in to ensure the wool was of good quality and met the monastery's high standards for selling the wool on. If a tenant farmer provided poor quality wool, he could find his future in jeopardy as the monastery would be unlikely to endorse him again. If the monks introduced poor quality wool onto the market their reputation would be sullied so they carried out business dealings with the utmost professionalism.

In most of their business transactions the monks were the dominant partner; their inspections of their tenant farmers and business tasks were a serious part of their working day and an invaluable way to keep revenue coming into the monastery. As well as astute businessmen, the monks were also providers of basic medicine and benefactors to the poor, providing beds in the infirmary for the old and the sick and food and alms to the desperate.

STUDY

The third activity that took up a monk's time was study. Monks had to learn, and in time teach, reading and writing. They were regularly tested and assessed both within their monasteries and by external assessors, who would travel from institution to institution maintaining standards across the board. The importance of monks as writers and recorders can be seen throughout Britain and Ireland as many of our earliest texts are the result of their endeavours. It was their ability to record events in letters that has taught us so much about the time periods they lived in.

Monasteries could house libraries of great worth and the books contained within them were works of art, beautifully illustrated and written with the highest levels of calligraphy. The sacrist was the monk in charge of the books and parchments, and in maintaining the quality of the monastery's collection. The monks occupied a valuable position in society, almost as a go-between from the educated upper classes to the less-educated lower classes. Indeed, they profited from the ever-rising middle class of traders and merchantmen eager to develop their business skills through a better knowledge of letters and numbers.

A 15th-century monk copying a manuscript at his work table

It would be wrong to think of a monk's day in the same terms as a typical working one – there is no 'nine to five'. It is the act of prayer that really sets up the structure of a monk's existence, and differentiates it from a tenant farmer's day. Eight prayer sessions throughout the day and night would be fatiguing but necessary, in their belief to appease God. Regardless of indiscretions in some institutions, the monasteries were powerful religious centres and prayer was central to their way of life. The work they carried out was for the benefit of the monastery and the community as a whole. What benefited one, benefited the other; the monks ensured their existence through personal endeavour and made certain the tenant farmers worked just as hard as well. The act of studying meant that the monks occupied a unique place in society, responsible for developing and furthering knowledge and passing knowledge on to a burgeoning middle class.

Though not an easy life, monks ate comparatively well, were relatively safe and secure, had the opportunity to learn and study and did not suffer many of the hardships that the peasantry faced. If guaranteeing this life meant deeper devotion to God than most, then it was worth it.

LAY RELIGION

re- Reformation churches were different from 21st-century Church of England places of worship and subtly different, too, from those of modern Catholicism. While the outward appearance was familiar, arrangements and decorations within the buildings were suited to the religious observance of the day.

Few rood screens were simple physical dividers. Most were exquisitely carved and painted to inspire devotion

Perhaps the most noticeable difference was the amount of open space. Few churches were filled with pews, with most naves uncluttered places where people could kneel, stand and walk about. Stretching right across the church, separating the nave from the chancel (where the priest officiated) was a rood screen. The rood was a large 3D representation of the crucifixion of Christ: both it and the screen it sat on top of was usually wooden, elaborately carved and brightly painted. It provided a physical barrier between the nave and chancel, but was pierced with many openings to allow the congregation to see and hear what went on at the main altar.

The walls of the church formed another part of the religious experience, with images intended to help people deepen and strengthen their spiritual life

Along the side walls of the nave (often painted with biblical scenes) were located a number of side altars. Pulpits were present in some, but not the majority of churches, whilst both painted stone and wooden sculptures of saints, apostles and the holy family were common. Candles burned in several places about the church.

THE LAY PERSON AT CHURCH

Our parish church had neither pews nor pulpit but it did boast both an elaborately carved and painted rood screen and a number of devotional images upon the walls -- these acted as a focus for meditation, discussion of the Christian message and prayer. As ordinary laypeople the Church expected us to have a certain basic knowledge of the Christian faith and to partake in a number of services and practices. There was no single catechism to be learnt by heart as there was after the Reformation. Nonetheless, we were required to be familiar with the Creed, the Ten Commandments, the Paternoster (the Lord's Prayer), the Ave Maria, the seven works of mercy, the seven deadly sins, the seven virtues and the seven sacraments.

> ❝ DEVOTIONAL IMAGES ON THE WALLS ACTED AS A FOCUS FOR MEDITATION AND PRAYER ❞

Weekly attendance on Sunday for high mass was encouraged but it was necessary only to go to confession and take Holy Communion just once a year at Easter. The services of course were in Latin rather than English and preaching was an occasional rather than a regular occurrence. At Sunday mass, the main requirements for us as members of the laity were to pray quietly as the priest went through the Latin service: to stand when the gospel was read and as the host was elevated (this accompanied by the ringing of a bell so we would not miss the moment); to kneel and look up from our prayers to see the moment of transubstantiation; and to utter an elevation prayer with hands raised in celebration.

GETTING MORE INVOLVED

If that was the minimum requirement, many people looked for much more involvement. Those who could read and afford one of the new printed prayer books read a range of prayers rather than simply saying the Paternosters and Ave Marias prompted by their rosary beads. Sunday service, meanwhile, offered more participation to those who remained for the whole period of worship rather than just the mass. It began with the blessing of salt and water, which were then mixed and carried in procession round the church. The altars and congregation were sprinkled with the now holy water as the

le compte a parler Deulx et retourne a parler de Booz

Holy Communion was generally received once a year

procession made its way around the building. Next came the 'bidding of the bedes', a call to prayer in English asking the congregation to pray for those in authority, for those in danger, for the householder who supplied this week's holy loaf and for the dead of the parish. This was followed by the pax ceremony: the priest would kiss the dish upon which the host rested, the lip of the chalice in which the wine was kept and then kiss a pax (a disc, tablet or stick upon which a cross, lamb of God or other sacred symbol was carved). This pax was offered to everyone in the congregation to kiss, accompanied by prayers – these were in English, and asked for peace and deliverance from enemies.

The priest then moved into the chancel to perform the mass. This was partially seen by the congregation who remained in the nave on the other side of the rood screen. Once the mass was finished, a loaf of bread presented by one of the parishioners (there was a rota) was blessed, cut up and distributed among all who were present. This was reminiscent of Holy Communion, but with an important difference. When the priest performed mass, according to Catholic doctrine, the bread and wine that he used became the actual blood and flesh of Christ; the holy loaf handed around among the congregation on a normal Sunday was simply bread that had been blessed. Only at Easter, after confession and penance, would ordinary members of the congregation take the bread of Holy Communion along with the priest.

Religion is rather more than the performing of stipulated ceremonies, and there is every reason to believe that the ordinary people of Britain took their faith much further. This was a time of very little active dissent. There were moans and complaints about corrupt and lax priests, ridicule of some practices (especially indulgences) and discussions about reform, but the Church was one united force: no one had any inclination that it would ever be anything else. People were born and brought up in a society that had little reason to doubt the Church's teachings.

JOINING A GUILD

Many laypeople in the late 15th and early 16th century were active members of religious guilds. These guilds offered their members an enhanced funeral, prayers for their souls after death, an opportunity to become more

FITZHERBERT'S BOKE OF HUSBANDRY

One example of how far Christian teaching played a part in laypeople's lives can be found in Fitzherbert's Boke of Husbandry. This is a book about farming technique and yet religious practice is not just mentioned, but actually constitutes almost a quarter of the text. Whole chapters are devoted to why and how you should pray, the importance of not just going through the motions and how to lead a godly life.

involved in the religious life of the parish and added another element to the individual's social life.

Religious guilds were a form of religious organisation invented and run entirely by laypeople, not the Church. They were open to most respectable men and women of the community upon the payment of a modest annual fee. The poorest members of society could rarely afford to join, but although the guilds were biased towards the more substantial inhabitants, there were still some quite humble members. In towns it tended to be the merchants and artisans who joined rather than the labourers and apprentices; in the countryside it was the more prosperous or established farmers.

The guild members got together regularly to raise money, to distribute charity and to take advantage of the additional services that they had set up. Each guild generally set up a side altar in the parish church and provided suitable cloths, candlesticks, candles and equipment for saying mass. The older, longer established guilds could build up impressive stocks of high quality chalices, plates, embroideries and hangings, commissioning sculpture and painting to surround the altar. Many employed a priest full time, while others secured the part-time services of a member of the clergy. These priests were tasked to say mass at their altar during the week for the souls of their members past and present.

FEASTING AND FUN

Christianity, its teachings and its practices, permeated all aspects of life. People expected every meal to be accompanied by a short prayer and they were used to religion being central to most of their social occasions. The Church calendar offered many opportunities for feasting and fun: the Whitsun-ale saw the parish get together with food and drink to dance and play whilst raising money for the church funds; Palm Sunday processions ended in people pelting one another with cakes and flowers. Christmas was a time of twelve days' feasting with music and plays and dance, while Plough Monday, the first working day after Christmas, largely consisted of dragging a plough around the village demanding drink from the other villagers (though they also called at the church, lit a candle and called upon the priest to bless the plough).

> " PLOUGH MONDAY LARGELY CONSISTED OF DRAGGING A PLOUGH AROUND THE VILLAGE DEMANDING DRINK FROM THE OTHER VILLAGERS "

Most parishes celebrated their own particular saint's day with more processions, services, communal feasting and drinking. Then there were weddings and christenings, and even funerals called for both eating and drinking. Other church-centred merriment involved sports and games, maypole dancing, singing and music, competitions between young men and women and putting on plays and mock battles.

PETER

PALM SUNDAY

I sometimes feel as if Professor Ronald Hutton is pulling our legs. It's Palm Sunday and I find myself holding a wooden cross, dressed in the flowing robes of a prophet, complete with a fake beard. Having read a prophetic lesson in church and led a procession around the village and to the market place, I am now standing witness to a 'snowball and pillow' fight between the villagers. They are throwing unleavened bread and hitting each other with bits of greenery and flowers that are being scattered in the process.

This is Palm Sunday: a major celebration in the Church's calendar. One week before Easter Sunday, it represents a respite from the solemnity of Lent when cupboards are bare – not only to remember the 40 days that Jesus spent in the desert, but also because this is the period of the farming calendar known as the 'hunger gap', with stores running low and new crops yet to emerge.

As bizarre as this may seem and as jovial as it was to participate in, Palm Sunday was still a very serious celebration. The layperson dressed as a prophet was particular to southern England it seems and is only recorded from the 1490s, though that doesn't mean it wasn't happening elsewhere or earlier. The fancy dress was there to add a bit of theatrics to the prophetic lessons. The idea wasn't to mock but to enhance what was being said. A popular prophet to dress up as was John the Baptist, depicted as he must have looked when he emerged from the wilderness. There are accounts of wigs and beards being made or even hired in. We made our beard from sheep's wool.

It is I, John the Baptist!

> **❝ I FIND MYSELF HOLDING A WOODEN CROSS, DRESSED IN THE FLOWING ROBES OF A PROPHET, COMPLETE WITH A FAKE BEARD ❞**

MONSTRANCES

Often on Palm Sunday the priests would lead a procession with a monstrance in order to bless the fields for a good harvest. A monstrance is usually in the shape of a sun with a small glass case at the centre. Inside this, the host would be held in place by a luna, meaning the blessed sacrament was on display with the sun and the moon.

The priest would never touch the monstrance with his flesh once the host was inside. Instead he would handle it wearing a humeral veil. This procession around the fields was important, as a blessing from the monstrance is seen as a blessing directly from Christ.

Whatever your views are about God and religion one thing is certain: this was a community event at the start of what was hopefully better weather. A bit of positive thinking can be extremely beneficial to a group of people whose very lives depend upon how well their crops do.

Leading our parish down to the market square for their 'snowball and pillow' fight

THE RELIGIOUS CALENDAR

 **D**uring the Middle Ages and up until the point of the dissolution of the monasteries a popular manuscript was the Book of Hours. Usually handwritten and sometimes ornately decorated and illuminated, the book of hours outlined the religious festivals that occurred during the year.

There were a number of feast days in the Book of Hours but some would have been more important than others. The most important were, and still are, known as holy days of obligation. It was expected that you would observe these days. It is from holy day that we get holiday.

Some of the principal feast days in the Tudor calendar were:

FEAST OF MARY THE BLESSED VIRGIN
1ST JANUARY

The first of the Marian feasts celebrating Mary.

ASH WEDNESDAY
40 DAYS BEFORE EASTER

The beginning of Lent. This day is a reminder that humans are made of dust and will return to dust, marked by 40 days of fasting.

PALM SUNDAY
SUNDAY BEFORE EASTER

The beginning of Holy Week. This celebrates Jesus's arrival in Jerusalem. The palms are burnt to make the ashes for the following year's Ash Wednesday. In Tudor England, a procession around the village was made led by a member of the community dressed as a prophet who also did a reading in the church (see page 46).

MAUNDY THURSDAY

The day that the three holy oils are blessed. These are the chrism oil, the oil of catechumens and the oil of the sick. The mass that is said remembers the Last Supper and the arrest and trial of Jesus. At the end of mass the altar is stripped, the statues are covered and the tabernacle is laid bare.

GOOD FRIDAY	No mass is said on this day. The ceremony includes kissing the feet of Jesus on the cross and celebrates the passion of Christ.
EASTER SUNDAY	*Lumen Christi, Deo Gratias.* This is the end of Lent and the celebration of Christ's resurrection.
ASCENSION DAY 40 DAYS AFTER EASTER	This is when the 'beating of bounds' takes place (see page 60).
PENTECOST 50 DAYS AFTER EASTER	This is the celebration of the Holy Spirit.
TRINITY SUNDAY ONE WEEK AFTER PENTECOST	This feast celebrates the Holy Trinity: the Father, the Son and the Holy Spirit.
CORPUS CHRISTI THURSDAY AFTER TRINITY SUNDAY	This feast celebrates the body and blood of Jesus Christ.
ASSUMPTION OF MARY 15TH AUGUST	This celebrates the rising of Mary into heaven.
ALL SAINTS' DAY 1ST NOVEMBER	The day after Hallowe'en (or Hallowed Eve).
FIRST SUNDAY OF ADVENT FOURTH SUNDAY BEFORE CHRISTMAS DAY	Like Lent, Advent involved fasting, with worshippers abstaining from meat for the duration.
IMMACULATE CONCEPTION 8TH DECEMBER	Celebrating the conception of Mary and the idea that she was free from sin.
CHRISTMAS DAY 25TH DECEMBER	Celebrating the birth of Christ.

Tom's Diary

MIDSUMMER'S EVE

Midsummer's Eve, a celebration of the summer solstice was a fantastic experience and one that really summed up both the Tudor period and Tudor farming. It was known to Tudor folk as the celebration of the feast of John the Baptist, and was one of the most important feast days of the year. As a celebration it involves Christianity, paganism, ale, dancing, socialising and fire... what's not to like? Added to this was Professor Hutton's statement that I would be carried off by my fairy mistress that night! Even if no one else was, I was ready to commit to a little paganism...

The three fires had their own purposes for being and in our case that meant one for drinking and dancing beside, one for jumping over and one where I had to throw the butchered remains of dead animals on to scare away dragons.

The first fire was the biggest and, despite it being a summer's night, it needed to be. A strong breeze was working its way up the valley and with some light showers meant that midsummer was not as summery as it could have been. The combination of the fire, the warm buzz of the ale and the simple but effective dance that Ruth introduced us to ensured we kept high spirits. The dance was effectively a Tudor conga-line with a little stretching thrown in, but its simplicity meant that we could all get involved without the need for tutelage. As with most simple things in life, when it went wrong it proved to be the most fun.

The second fire – to jump over – was our test of nerve. Though not a large fire, certain factors combined to make it more challenging. Firstly, a few ales could easily impair one's judgement. The length of the fire, the right place to jump from and the slope the fire was built on were but a few considerations. Secondly, the wet grass and the state of our grip-less boots added a little jeopardy. Everyone enjoys a pratfall, but no one wants to be the prat who tries to jump a fire, slips and lands in the flames. However, Ruth and Professor Hutton showed us the way. I followed and Peter chose the narrowest angle with which to jump. He was inspiring.

Our final fire, the 'bone-fire', was a medium-sized one with a single purpose: to ward off the aforementioned dragons. I have never smelt burning bone before thankfully and although I cannot vouch that it removed the threat of a dragon attack (although admittedly we were not attacked by one) it was a good way to bring the celebrations to an end. The roaring fire soon crumbled the bone, the flames soon turned greasy with the fat of rotting flesh and our guests soon departed in search of more cordial entertainment.

One of the most fascinating things about religion is the way later ones are deeply rooted in earlier practices. Midsummer's Eve was the perfect example of a Christian people reaching back and recognising the power and centrality of nature to their lives and livelihoods. I loved the duality of it all and yet was disappointed for two reasons: no beautiful fairy mistress came for me and no dragon either graced or terrified us with its presence. Surely every boy hopes to see at least one dragon in their lifetime, and at least two or three beautiful fairy mistresses!

AROUND
THE FARM

In Tudor England the Church owned most of the land. If you were a farmer, the chances were you would have been working on soil controlled by a monastery.

Although the Church could evict farmers who were not up to scratch or weren't producing enough crops or wool, it wasn't a simple case of the monasteries being able to dictate terms and take a cut of the produce. The majority of farmers paid a rent, and while crops grown favoured the interests of the monasteries, it was largely because that was the market and was a case of fulfilling demand.

OPEN FIELD SYSTEM

PETER

The open field system, also known as the three field system, was the primary form of farming in use in Britain up until the enclosure acts of the 18th and 19th centuries. Centred around a village, three huge fields were divided up into long strips and the land was allocated, usually by drawing lots, among the villagers. This was to ensure that there was a fair division of both good and bad land between the recipients.

Villagers appraising our sheep at the market

Not all of Britain had this system: parts of counties such as Kent and Essex still had enclosed fields left over from when the Romans were farming. However, the majority of the land in Britain was being farmed using the open field system.

The fields consisted of hundreds of acres of land and in order to successfully farm them the villagers had to work together. Each village usually had three fields (giving the 'three fields system' its name) and they would rotate the crops year on year. One field would contain a white crop such as wheat or barley, which would be planted prior to the winter. A second field would have a crop such as peas or beans that fixed nitrogens in the soil and improved the land. This crop was planted in the spring so the work was staggered throughout the year. The final field was left fallow. This was an improvement on the two field system where one field had a crop and the other field was left fallow.

UPS AND DOWNS

The fields weren't fenced in, hence the term 'open'. One problem with this, coupled with the sheer size of the fields, was that animals could stray onto the land and roam around, trampling and eating crops. In terms of their own animals, the villagers had access to common lands where these could graze, meadows where they could cut hay and woodlands where they could keep their pigs. There was usually also a village green for communal gatherings and celebrations.

" ONE PROBLEM WITH THIS SYSTEM WAS THAT ANIMALS COULD STRAY ONTO THE LAND, TRAMPLING AND EATING CROPS "

Perhaps unsurprisingly, many cases have been recorded of villagers trying to swap their strip allocations around so that they ended up with land that was parcelled together: this can really be seen as the start of enclosure. Changes in the profitability of sheep farming also led to farmland being enclosed and by the Tudor period it was a political hot potato, with Henry VII's parliament passing acts to stop enclosure.

A view of the village centre through open fields

When the dissolution of the monasteries occurred, all that land that had previously been owned by the Church got divided up amongst the elite

RIDGES AND FURROWS

Villagers would band together to plough their strips with teams of oxen. A team of oxen has quite a large turning circle, so it is beneficial to keep them ploughing in a straight line for as long as possible. The ploughing of these fields, year in year out, created deep ridges and tall furrows that can be seen in the landscape today. I wonder if the ridges and furrows were extenuated by the villagers as it gave a good demarcation of the various strips that each person was farming and also meant that there was a straight line for the oxen to follow when they were ploughing.

Ruth shows the two beasts – and the cows – how to plough

of society to ensure their support for the changes being made, and many people lost their rights to land that they had been farming for generations. This was the final nail in the coffin of the open field system. When enclosure finally did happen, allotments began to be established instead. This was a way to offer land back to the poor of the parish, with the oldest allotment thought to be the Great Somerford Free Gardens in Wiltshire, secured in 1809 by the village rector.

A HISTORICAL FOOTNOTE?

It is very easy to dismiss the open field system as a footnote in farming history. The focus is usually on the agricultural revolutions of the 18th and 19th centuries, starting with Jethro Tull's seed drill of 1701.

> " VILLAGERS HAD TO WALK LONG DISTANCES TO FIRSTLY GET TO THEIR ALLOCATED PLOTS OF LAND AND THEN WALK FURTHER IN BETWEEN THE PLOTS OF LAND "

Tudor life demonstrating the evolution of the horse collar

It is true that the three field system did have its disadvantages. It was hard to control the breeding of your animals as they roamed on the common land with the other animals. Villagers had to walk long distances to firstly get to their allocated plots of land and then walk further in between the plots of land. This may not sound too hard but if you are doing it day in day out, you are wasting a lot of time, not to mention carrying tools and any food or drink that you need for the day. There was little farmers could do against the spread of weeds and wildflowers, and the scope to experiment either with crops or farming practices was limited as the whole village was working together.

However, compared to the land being divided up as political bribes in the 16th century, the open field system was a relatively fair form of agriculture. This is a system that endured for centuries and in certain parts of the United Kingdom it is still going. The most famous example is that of the village of Laxton in Nottinghamshire, which still has three commonly farmed open fields – Mill Field, South Field and West Field. Although the allocation of land has increased to mirror changes in farming methods such as tractors, essentially this is a piece of medieval history that remains unchanged.

BEATING THE BOUNDS

PETER

 **I**f you can imagine early Tudor England with its open fields and very few land boundaries such as hedges or fences, then the ceremony of beating the bounds was an important one. Land charters of the time could be very vague and the delineation of parishes could be unclear: the existence of material maps was rare and obviously there were no high-tech GPS systems to pinpoint exact land limitations. Beating the bounds was a way to ensure that all the parishioners knew exactly what constituted someone's land and what they were responsible for. It created an intangible communal folk memory map that endured as long as the ceremony was carried out.

Beating the bounds generally happened on the day of the festival of Ascension. The priest would lead the parishioners armed with freshly cut green sticks and branches around the boundary markers of the parish. As the party went round, everyone would hit the objects that they essentially had to remember: so if one boundary was from the large rock on the hill to the oak tree in the bottom of the valley, these items and this boundary would be struck with the sticks.

Unfortunately for the younger members of the parish, they too would often be beaten with the sticks at various markers or have their heads knocked against the relevant objects to make sure that they remembered the route. At significant places, hymns would be sung and readings from the gospel would be undertaken by the priest – this is where Gospel Oak in North London gets its name from. As the boundaries were generally around the extent of the farmland, it was thought that the ceremony would also ensure a good harvest.

Beating the bounds dates from the Anglo-Saxon period but there is evidence to suggest that the Romans undertook a similar ceremony to celebrate the god Terminus, who protected boundary markers. To make sure that the parishioners turned up year on year a 'parish-ale' was held at the end of the ceremony. By the reign of Henry VIII these parish-ales (otherwise known as a very good party) were rumoured to be completely debauched.

Although the practical need for the ceremony is no longer necessary, beating the bounds

Our friend and mentor, Professor Ronald Hutton

is still carried out in various parts of the country. In Sussex we were joined by our old friend Professor Ronald Hutton to beat the bounds of our surrounding parish.

We went up Levin Down, adjacent to our farm, and which is still managed as a nature reserve, preserving its state as a medieval landscape. Subsequently it is a haven for a diverse range of plants and wildflowers, butterflies, grasshoppers and other insects, and beating the bounds through it was not only a way to mark our territory, but a beautiful way to take stock of the farm and really appreciate our lands.

THE PEA CROP

PETER **p**eas and beans were a very important source of carbohydrates before the availability of rice, pasta and potatoes. They are also a good source of protein, which was important at a time when meat could be expensive or scarce depending on your situation. We might associate peas and beans with gardening but in the past they were a field crop, and we were going to grow them.

We decided to grow the variety of pea known as carlin peas. Often when we embark on these projects, we can find it hard to get hold of good seed stock but there are plenty of carlin peas around. They are certainly recorded as being consumed in the reign of Elizabeth I and it is thought that they originated in the gardens of the monasteries. They have a strong association with the north of England and are certainly a vegetable to be celebrated. Did I say vegetable? I meant fruit: peas are technically fruit because the pod grows from a flower and has seeds inside.

PLANTING

After we had worked our ground, it was time to sow. There were many benefits to sowing a crop of peas: firstly they don't take very long to grow; secondly they are legumes, meaning that they get their nitrates from the air so can grow in poor soil (they will however fix nitrates in the soil, leaving the ground ready for a white crop such as wheat); and thirdly, they can be sown thickly. Basically, we could carpet the area with peas and they would do well. You can even sow a later crop on top of the one growing in order to stagger when the peas mature. This worked well for us because we were sowing by hand.

I didn't know you could read!

Broadcast sowing is erratic. It is accepted that crops do well if they are fairly regular, hence the invention of the seed drill. This meant that each plant had an equal amount of soil, making it possible to weed between the rows as the plants come up. This is most important at the early stages of growth. If the crop can get above the weeds then it will have the light: if the weeds get above, then the crop is in trouble.

Luckily for us our peas were very quick off the mark due to a change in weather.

One Tudor writer, Gervase Markham, in his book *Cheape and Good Husbandry* stated that the best way to broadcast sow is to put one foot forward while taking a handful of peas, then throwing them when the other foot goes forward. It sounds easy, but it's a bit like rubbing your tummy while patting your head – it is possible and it isn't that hard, but it takes a little practice.

We only had one wooden hopper which Tom was using, so I opted to use my hat. This was a bit of a mistake as we had taken the decision to soak the peas overnight before sowing them. My felt hat was very good at keeping rain off my head, but was also, I discovered, very good at keeping pea water in.

Once we had satisfied ourselves that the field had an even covering of peas, we harrowed and rolled the field. Rolling is designed to keep the birds off the seeds. One of the major problems with growing peas is that once the birds have taken the uncovered seeds, they wait and

Our field – from brown to green to pea!

pretty soon there are tiny juicy green shoots, which if they pull will pop out of the ground attached to a nice pea. In Tudor England children with sticks would have fended off the birds.

It was only a few weeks until our crop started coming up. When the plants are more established the birds are no longer a problem. Instead, it is now the turn of the deer, the rabbits and the mice to have a go. I couldn't blame them: when I picked one of the young plants and ate it, it was divine. You sometimes see pea shoots and tops for sale and I can only say they make the best salads. Unfortunately, every living creature in a mile radius agreed. There was very little we could do and our struggles gave a good insight into the mindset of a Tudor farmer.

HARVESTING

One of my major worries regarding the pea crop was just exactly how we were going to harvest it. In my mind I saw days of backbreaking pea picking, but the Tudor solution was much simpler. Although like a sweet pea (and I'm sure the garden ones were eaten fresh), the carlin pea was dried and kept for cooking throughout the year. To harvest, therefore, we scythed and rolled the crop into bundles and took it to our barn to dry. When it was ready we hit it bundle by bundle with flails over a large cloth. We stored the vegetable matter for animal fodder and the peas for the kitchen.

DIVINE INTERVENTION?
One text we came across that sparked debate was an account (written by an atheist) that stated that farmers would smuggle the *panis benedictus* out of the mass and sprinkle the bread on the field. This is the blessed bread, not the Eucharist – that would have been sacrilege and an offence punishable both in the eyes of God and by the laws of man. Whether this happened or not one thing is certain; the sheer helplessness that is felt when a crop is in the ground is timeless.

Tom's Diary

BROADCAST SOWING A PEA CROP

Broadcast sowing was something that I took to very easily. Taking responsibility for our arable crop was no little thing but there are various steps one can take to manage the risk of a poor crop.

Firstly, one has to have a plentiful supply of seeds because there will always be loss due to natural interventions: birds, rabbits, deer and bad weather to name but a few. Secondly, one must broadcast efficiently. The secret to good broadcasting is to fling the seeds evenly in an arc in front of you. That way, when you walk back on your return journey down the field the coverage of seeds over the ground is comprehensive. Luckily, a carlin pea once soaked is large enough to be easily visible as one walks up and down, and when the seeds germinated and the crop started to grow one could easily see how well broadcast sowing worked. In the end, we were able to grow enough plants to intentionally feed ourselves and unintentionally the birds, the deer and the rabbits.

We were, thankfully, able to complete the sowing without becoming 'haperised'. This is a Tudor term for the sowers becoming doubled up by having the weight of the 'hopper' – the box the peas were held in – pulling them forward. That said, you could feel your core muscles working as you tried to maintain your posture. It brought home the fact that even a relatively low-level physical activity like sowing could, through repetition, drastically – and permanently – damage one's health in Tudor times.

WOODLAND MANAGEMENT

PETER

I n the Tudor period, managing the woodlands was of paramount importance. Trees were in demand as a supply of timber for building to house an increasing population and as a supply of fuel to meet the demands of new industries such as iron smelting. Equally the woodlands were being eyed up as potential pasture land. Every inch of Tudor woodland would have had a purpose and every tree had to be looked after in accordance with a long-term plan.

HISTORY

Wildwood is a term coined by the ecologist Oliver Rackham. It denotes the unmanaged tree growth in Britain that occurred between the end of the last ice age 13,000 years ago and 4,000 years ago when the wildwood was fully established.

The process began once the ice had cleared: seeds blew in on the wind or were carried by birds or animals. The first species of trees to take root in what would become a temperate zone with a maritime climate were arctic trees like aspen, birch and willow. These were followed by pine, hazel, alder and oak. Then came elm and lime and finally ash, holly, hornbeam and maple (a temperate zone and maritime climate means that the ocean to the west regulates the temperature so that there is little difference between the coldest winter and the hottest summer; in a continental climate, winter and summer are poles apart).

Around about 6,000 years ago, about the start of what we class as the British Neolithic period, it is estimated that the clearance and management of the wildwood began. Timber was used to build houses and for fuel, tools, boats and so forth; land, meanwhile, was needed to grow crops and rear animals. Woodlands that were used for grazing livestock were known as wood pasture but one effect was that the grazing prevented

The ins and outs of a wattle fence

Wattle fencing not only created a barrier for animals, it was also a supply of seasonal firewood when it was replaced

low level re-growth. By the time of the Norman Conquest, much of the woodland had been cleared; by the reign of Henry VII any woodland was managed to ensure a supply of timber.

COPPICING

Perhaps the most well known of all woodland management systems is coppicing. Coppicing relies on the fact that most indigenous British trees will re-grow if cut at the base of the trunk. In coppiced woodland the new growth of the trees is repeatedly harvested, leaving the roots and a stump, known as a stool, from which this growth springs up. One of the characteristics of wood that has at one time been coppiced are straight poles ending in a curve – this is because the new shoots grow out the side of the stool and then bend up towards the light.

Coppiced woodland is generally managed on a cycle, so at any one time there is always wood at different growth stages. The length of the cycle

" AROUND ABOUT 6,000 YEARS AGO, THE CLEARANCE AND MANAGEMENT OF THE WILDWOOD BEGAN "

A halved joint in ash forming the upper corner of our pigsties

will depend upon both the type of tree (hazel may be seven years but oak may be as much as fifty) and also what the wood is needed for. One of the major uses of coppiced woodland during the Tudor period was for charcoal to use in iron and lead production. These woods were so important that Henry VIII saw fit to standardise and protect the practice.

When harvesting coppiced wood, it is important to leave a clean cut otherwise the tree will struggle to grow again. In woods where timber was being grown for use in shipbuilding or for equipment such as ploughs, the woodsmen would watch and know their trees. They would encourage the growth in a certain way over a period of decades so that when a particular piece of wood with a specific curve or grain pattern was needed, they could meet the demand.

Although coppicing still goes on in a few places commercially in this country, the skills, knowledge, time and patience that are required to produce the timbers of old are lacking. We are no longer men of wood, or men of stone: but are now men of glass, steel and plastic.

POLLARDING

Pollarding was a very popular system of tree management during the Tudor period. It is like coppicing but rather than cutting the trees back at the base of the plant, material is taken from higher up the trunk of the tree. This results in a tree trunk perhaps six or seven feet high with a shock of new growth almost like hair. The word poll means head and the term pollarding is thought to come from the idea that one is giving the tree a haircut.

" THE TERM POLLARDING IS THOUGHT TO COME FROM THE IDEA THAT ONE IS GIVING THE TREE A HAIRCUT "

Pollarding allows trees to be grown to a set height determined by the landowner. This can make them look quite ornate when viewed as a group. Usually, the height of the trunk was determined by the animals that were grazing in the area, to ensure that the new growth would be out of their reach. Pollarding, like coppicing, prolongs the life of a tree and pollarded trees are often found to be hollow. This makes sense when you think that the living parts of a tree are the bark, sapwood, branches and leaves.

Tom felling a self-seeded ash tree

As well as being pollarded to provide a source of wood, trees were also managed in this way to provide a source of fodder for animals. The growth of leafy material on top of a pollarded tree was excessively abundant if left for a couple of years: the trunk would be sucking up nutrients and water for a much larger tree, meaning all that growth was directed at the foliage. This was known as tree hay.

It is only recently that grass, as either hay or silage, has become the foremost, almost solitary, foodstuff for livestock. Certainly before much of the wildwood was cleared, trees would have been a primary, if un-managed, nutrient source. One of the major benefits of tree hay is that it can be cut in the rain, so if you have a poor summer all is not lost. Furthermore animals could be allowed to graze the grass around the pollarded trees, helping enrich the soil.

SHREDDING, SNEDDING AND SNAGGING

The term shredding may be where we get the term snedding from – the practice of removing side branches from the tree once it has been felled. Sometimes this is also called snagging, which is now what builders do at the end of a job in order to tidy everything up.

SHREDDING

Very similar to pollarding is the ancient practice of shredding. This is where all side branches were periodically removed from a tree, leaving only a growth at the top of a very long trunk. The branches that were removed could be used for fuel and the trunk of the tree would hopefully have a straight grain and relatively few incidental knots.

Examples of shredded trees

Perhaps due to its similarity to pollarding and coppicing, there is little evidence that shredding continued much beyond the Middle Ages in Britain.

Tom's Diary

COPPICING

Coppicing is a traditional rural activity going back centuries in this country. It has taken place in the British Isles since ancient times – the Romans did it to mass produce charcoal and the Anglo-Saxons coppiced to mass produce a ready supply of purposely-sized timbers for their home-building. It is as viable now as a commercial concept as it ever was and yet it is rarely practised anymore.

We followed that coppicing tradition with our pigsty and fences. I have done it before but to have someone of John's calibre alongside will always be of benefit. John took me to an area where the hazel had grown to a practical size for our wattle fencing and this emphasised how simple a concept coppicing was. Good woodland management was the only requirement, and with that in place, one can harvest workable wood supplies over a continual nine-year cycle in different areas of the wood. Effective woodland management also means you know exactly where to go to get the right size wood for a specific project. Really one only has to rely on nature to do its thing and you have a constant supply of working materials throughout the year, year after year.

INSIDE THE DAIRY

RUTH

Calm and quiet, airy and cool, the dairy was one of my favourite places throughout our Tudor sojourn. I enjoyed the work involved here, meeting the needs of various enzymes and bacteria cultures, adjusting temperatures, humidity levels and acidity balances, and developing flavours and textures. Dairies have always felt to me like places outside the usual hustle and bustle of life, but even so, this one was special.

Look at that big grin! I find dairy work so enjoyable

With the northern light falling on the lime-washed walls and the soft, visual texture of the well-scrubbed wooden shelves and utensils, the dairy made for a beautiful setting. The through draught, meanwhile, brought in the scents of the garden to mingle with the clean earth smell that rose from the porous tiles.

The dairy was a cleverly designed space, built to do a very specific job. Milk, cheese, butter and cream are delicate foodstuffs, and they can be spoiled and rendered unfit for consumption if they are not produced and kept in exactly the right conditions. Modern dairies address these challenges with acres of stainless steel, steam cleaners, thermometers and refrigeration. The butter and cheese makers of 1500 didn't have these options and solved these problems utilising the technologies of the day.

> ❝ MILK, CHEESE, BUTTER AND CREAM ARE DELICATE FOODSTUFFS, AND THEY CAN BE SPOILED AND RENDERED UNFIT FOR CONSUMPTION IF THEY ARE NOT PRODUCED AND KEPT IN EXACTLY THE RIGHT CONDITIONS ❞

THE DAIRY BUILDING

Architecture was the key. In order to protect against the heat of summer and the frosts of winter, regulate humidity and inhibit bacterial growth, where and how you built your dairy was crucial. A good dairy was part of a range of structures, located on the north-eastern corner. This allowed the other buildings to provide a degree of insulation from the sun: a stand-alone unit would have experienced the direct rays upon its southern and western walls, heating the interior. Windows in my dairy were located on both the north- and east-facing exposed walls. Little direct sunlight could penetrate but lots of air could be encouraged to flow freely through the room. That was important: dairies, due both to the liquid nature of the milk and the extensive hygiene regime, are wet places. Harmful moulds and bacteria thrive in damp humid conditions, so a good strong draught of fresh air plays an important part in keeping the space as dry as possible.

Where possible, those who specialised in dairying liked to divert a small stream through the building, down the centre of the room; archaeology has revealed various buildings with this feature and there are still some surviving Devon farmhouse dairies that retain the gutter. A supply of permanently running cold water was not only very convenient for cleaning, but kept the room perfectly cool.

SHELVING

Where an integral stream could not be arranged in a dairy, further temperature control could be achieved by fitting two different types of shelving: wooden and stone. In the early spring, when frost threatened, wooden shelves provided a little insulation from the worst cold, and in conjunction with a woollen cover could keep milk from freezing or chilling too quickly. In the summer, stone shelving held down the temperature of anything placed upon it. Further cooling could be achieved by wetting down the shelves daily.

Different types of stone shelving had different advantages and the most well equipped dairies would have more than one type of shelving. Where dairy products were in direct contact with the shelving, close-grained stone was preferred for cleanliness. For temperature, however, porous stone was best. The best dairies would have a slate or other non-permeable stone for keeping butter and cheese, and a separate limestone or sandstone area upon which dishes of milk and cream could be stood.

Scrubbed with salt and scalded with boiling water, the dairy was kept scrupulously clean

My dairy did not have a stream running through it, but it did have a tiled floor. The tiles were unglazed and porous. They could hold water and allow for its gradual evaporation throughout the day, driven by the draught from my two north and easterly windows. This kept the temperature low and steady throughout the hottest day.

In essence, the architecture provided me with a simple-to-operate refrigerated space. Each morning before I began work in the dairy, I emptied a bucket of water over my dairy floor and spread it out with a broom. With the pores of the tiles all saturated with water, any spills or splashes of milk or cream that fell on it during the day did not sink in. They remained floating upon the surface and at the end of the day, I threw down a second bucketful of water, brushing the dirt and excess liquid out in one easy operation.

DAIRY HYGIENE

Dairymaids were only too aware that milk goes off easily, poor hygiene made disgusting tasting butter and cheese, and that sickness followed eating corrupted food. The earliest written advice on how to achieve the right levels of dairy cleanliness was not printed until 1589, but the practice was already hundreds of years old and involved a combination of scalding water, salt, air and sunlight.

All dairy utensils and working surfaces were regularly scrubbed with salt and scalded with boiling water. They were then thoroughly dried by being placed in strong air currents. Modern science shows us that this is a highly effective regime. Bacteria do not like a salty environment, slowing their growth and in many cases killing them off. The scrubbing, meanwhile, removes traces of food that they might feed upon. Any bacteria remaining would be killed by the flood of boiling water that followed. Of course, bacteria like damp conditions so allowing vessels to stand wet for any length of time could lead to problems. Air-drying in a strong current of fresh air therefore also served a useful purpose.

" SOAP WAS AVOIDED AS EVEN THE FAINTEST TRACES LEFT ITS FLAVOUR IN DAIRY PRODUCE "

Early dairywomen had one final hygiene trick up their sleeves – sunlight. It was well known that allowing clean tubs, dishes and churns to stand in sunlight kept them 'sweet', preventing moulds or a frowsty smell. Again, the dairymaids were ahead of the scientists: we are now aware that UV light is an effective killer not only of many moulds and mildews, but also of bacteria. One thing that wasn't used in the hygiene process was soap. This was avoided as even the faintest trace left its flavour in dairy produce. The same went for those basic standby chemicals of medieval and Tudor cleaning: ammonia bleach derived from urine and sodium potassium derived from wood ash. Like soap, they left their mark upon dairy produce, making them unpalatable.

A well-built and well-kept dairy was both clean and cool and benefited from a careful selection of wooden and earthenware utensils and a variety of shelving options. By employing warm, boiling or cold water and wrapping vessels in linen or wool cloths, temperatures could be fine-tuned and held steady, whatever the weather conditions and the needs of the various dairy processes.

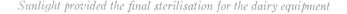

Sunlight provided the final sterilisation for the dairy equipment

MAKING CHEESE

Monasteries were famous throughout the medieval period for their sheep's milk cheeses. Whilst the milk yield from ewes is tiny in comparison to that of cows (only around a tenth), the huge flocks run by monks for their wool offered a substantial by-product. As lambing came to a close, shepherds had a brief few days to gather their strength, and their pots and pans, before the milking season began.

The usual rule of good husbandry was that a lamb should be left to suck for its first ten days unhindered; from then on, it was considered strong enough to share its mother's milk with the shepherd. Milking an average flock of 60 or so ewes every day was hard work and one that required several people, not to mention a good relationship between sheep and human; all mammals have difficulty letting down their milk if they are stressed or nervous. When the ewe is relaxed and used to the procedure, however, it can give up to a pint in around 15 minutes.

RENNET

For every ten ewes in milk, one lamb has to be sacrificed to produce the rennet that changes milk into cheese. The shepherd selects one that looks less vigorous than the rest, and while the remainder of the meat goes to the pot, the stomach is sent to the dairy. The inner membrane of a young mammal's stomach produces rennet – an enzyme that splits milk into solid curds and liquid whey.

The summer months are cheese-making season

The age of the chosen lamb is crucial: enzyme production doesn't get going until the lamb has begun to suckle, and after the first meal or two of colostrums has been taken; once the young animal begins to eat solid food those enzymes change, so it is important to slaughter the lamb before it is weaned.

The stomach is cleaned inside and out and all other membranes and traces of fat or muscle are removed. This can be a smelly job, although not as unpleasant as dealing with a stomach that has been consuming solid food. Next, the stomach is salted to prevent decay setting in, with generous handfuls rubbed in. The membrane is then stretched and allowed to dry over several days until it looks like a piece of parchment.

I have done this a number of times, but as with the milking, this was the first time

It takes the milk from 20 sheep to make such a cheese

❝ **WHEN THE EWE IS RELAXED AND USED TO THE PROCEDURE, IT CAN GIVE UP TO A PINT IN AROUND 15 MINUTES** ❞

I'd done so with a sheep. Slaughtering such a young animal is never pleasant and there have been many attempts over the years to find other substances to turn the milk. Whether experiments in early history were motivated by sentiment or necessity, there are references as early as the Anglo-Saxon era (pre-1066) that some people employed a number of herbs for the purpose. Stinging nettles, sorrel and goosegrass or cleavers are mentioned, and they do all work to a degree. The amount of cheese that results from a given amount of milk is very disappointing, however, and often less than half the amount that you get from using rennet.

CHEESE MAKING

With milk and rennet in the dairy, cheese making can begin. First a piece of rennet-bag is cut from the rest and put into some warm water to soak. Next, the milk is 'siled' or strained to make sure there are no specks of dirt or hair in it. Milk can be blended at this stage to make different styles of cheese: some cheese is made with milk from a single milking session; others come from today's and yesterday's milk which allows for larger batches and a more developed flavour (the nature of yesterday's milk will have begun gently to change under the influences of the enzymes and bacteria present).

Many modern cheese makers working with pasteurised milk actually add 'starter cultures' of specific helpful bacteria at this stage, as the natural mix is killed by the pasteurisation process. A Tudor dairymaid, by contrast, simply had to let nature do its work. If an exceptionally rich and creamy cheese was wanted for example, milk could be blended with cream made the previous day; a thin form of cheese could be made from milk that the cream had been skimmed off from. Once you were happy with the blend, the

milk must be raised to blood temperature to allow the rennet to work at maximum efficiency. Most dairymaids would put the milk in a pan over the fire, keeping a careful eye and stirring regularly to prevent it from catching or becoming 'scalded'. This is the method that I usually use. You can also add hot water to the milk instead: this avoids the

Once pressed, the cheese is rubbed with salt to create a rind

dangers of too much heat, but gives you much bigger volumes of liquid to deal with. Once the temperature is right, the rennet water is mixed in and the milk is left to stand.

CURDS AND WHEY... AND CHEESE

Ideally, the tub should remain at blood heat for about half an hour. If the weather is cold, using wooden tubs stood on a wooden shelf, carefully wrapped in a woollen blanket is advised. The rennet should then have set the milk into a curd, which can be gently cut with a knife or your hand to release the watery whey. If you have achieved a good

strong set, it should be possible to drain off a quantity of whey, gently scooping the remaining curds to one side of the tub – their own weight will squeeze out more whey without breaking the curd structure. After around half an hour of such drainage, the cottage-cheese-like curd can be transferred into a cloth, hung up and allowed to drain further overnight.

The following day the cloth-hung curd can be taken down, spread in a clean tub and a generous handful of salt sprinkled and mixed in. A clean cloth is wetted, wrung out and placed into a mould as the salted curd is piled in. The cloth is then folded over the curd and a wooden 'follower' is put on top. The mould is then set somewhere to continue to drain. Later in the day, a weight is added on top of the mould – around five pounds or three kilos is good for a six-inch-diameter, three-inch-deep cheese. In the days that

Soon the shelves will begin to fill with ripening cheeses

" YOU CAN, OF COURSE, EAT IT AT ANY STAGE OF PRODUCTION "

follow, the cheese is wiped over with a solution of salt water and laid upon a wooden shelf, often on a bed of fresh green rush stems, turning it each time.

You can, of course, eat it at any stage of production. However, such a cheese is usually best at around a month old and unlikely to remain tasty for more than six months.

THE ANIMALS

Farming was very much about community: open fields, common grazing land and shared oxen to do the heavy work. It was also a profession that was at the cutting edge of many technologies that were coming to Britain.

This was a time that was about to see huge change. Growing towns placed a demand on the countryside for meat, which in turn led to changes in sheep farming and stock control. More importantly, the church's power was about to be wrenched away from it, and their land divided up. But as yet, the farmers had no clue of this – as far as they were concerned it was Merry Old England…

WORKING WITH LIVESTOCK

TOM

The variety of livestock that played a part on the Tudor farm was extensive. These animals and birds all had different purposes but helped link the Tudor farm into the bigger market economy. Their centrality to Tudor life can not be underestimated and when one animal's importance waned another rose up to take its place; such as the decline of the sheep and the rise of the pig.

Any animal kept on a Tudor farm was there to fulfil a role of service: we dealt with working animals for the simple reason that farmers of the time did not have the luxury of pets. If we, as Tudor farmers, were going to keep animals, it meant that we would have to feed, shelter and care for them. That entailed an outlay of time, cost and effort, which the animals had to repay.

" IF WE WERE GOING TO KEEP ANIMALS, IT MEANT AN OUTLAY OF TIME, COST AND EFFORT, WHICH THE ANIMALS HAD TO REPAY "

Working with livestock can be divided into three categories; those that were a pleasure to work with; those with whom working was tolerable; and those I would work with out of pure necessity, and for no other reason.

DOGS AND HORSES

The animals that were a pleasure to work with were the dogs and horses. The affinity one can build with an animal will always be a source of intrigue and joy and that affinity comes so easily with these creatures.

Sparky, our packhorse, really grew on me. When first told that I would be the one responsible for Sparky, I was delighted. Then we tried to manoeuvre Sparky through narrow pathways with all our gear loaded up on his back and a lot of people around. Sparky was far from happy: he could only be described as an independent thinker and he did not feel the need to toe the line! However, the more time we spent together, the happier Sparky and I became in each other's company, and the more compliant he

Sparky finally signified his acceptance of me by licking my face. A beautiful animal, but a very wet tongue!

The sheep were the most nervous of our animals

became to my commands. Soon, Sparky was turning on a sixpence, going up and down steep slopes and more than comfortable in crowds of people. His natural curiosity in what we were up to made him almost the fourth member of our group.

Bess, our bearded collie, was a genuine working animal and one of the biggest characters I worked with. She had a heritage going back to Tudor times, although of Scottish origin, and her contemporaries down in the south of England would have looked and worked in a similar way. A dog like Bess was used to control the sheep and would have worked in tandem with a larger, stronger dog such as a mastiff: this would have been used to fend off wolves, other dogs and strangers that threatened the shepherd and the flock.

Bess had a lighter bodyweight than a mastiff and the endurance to cover long distances. She worked long hours and her amazingly placid temperament meant that

I never feared for the safety of the sheep. That said, watching her track our sheep was like watching a lion stalk her prey. Bess would focus on the sheep and then drop her shoulders, keeping low to the ground but moving with surprising speed.

Dogs are meat eaters, and meat is – and certainly was – a precious commodity. If one is going to take meat off the family dinner table to feed an animal then that animal has to prove its worth. Fortunately, Bess' work rate totally justified her diet.

> **" IF ONE IS GOING TO TAKE MEAT OFF THE FAMILY DINNER TABLE TO FEED AN ANIMAL THEN THAT ANIMAL HAS TO PROVE ITS WORTH "**

Peter and Neil, our pigman, appraise the new addition to the farm: Turkish, the boar!

PIGS

The pigs were the surprise package for me. Having been warned of their aggressive disposition, we were apprehensive initially of working in or around the pigpen. However, we soon found that we could work in the area doing any fence repairs that we needed to do without any trouble at all. The wieners were akin to puppies in temperament and their constant curiosity with everything we did always made us smile.

One particularly dark haired wiener took to following me around and on a couple of occasions this gave me a bit of a fright. You must always be aware of a sow giving milk, and Peter and I never entered the pig enclosure without due care and noting the location of the pigs before we entered. Yet on two occasions, my nosy little friend would make his way through the undergrowth beneath my eye-line and appear behind me with a loud snort! Fearing the sow, I managed to clear the fence in one easy bound!

I was once told that when an abattoir worker looks at a pig, mentally dividing it up into bacon, sausages and chops, the pig itself is staring back thinking something very similar. And when we were working on the sty or fence repair, the wieners were more than happy to nibble at my boots and legs. Peter never suffered such trials: either he does not look as edible as

I do, or my Celtic/Viking appearance was something our Tamworth pigs thought they could relate to, with their reddish hair and propensity to burn in the sun.

These instances aside, the pigs were friendly, endearingly curious and did what we required of them; clearing ground by pannaging and going on to provide us with money and meat.

The pigs proved to be very sociable animals. After digging themselves a shallow dust bath, they liked nothing better than to bundle in on top of each other and take a well-deserved nap!

COWS AND SHEEP

Working with cows and sheep was less of a pleasure, because of their lack of curiosity. The dog, horse and pigs always seemed interested in why you were there or what you were up to. The cows, by contrast, had a kind of melancholy nonchalance to them. The sheep never seemed to completely trust us and one could sense their resentment from a mile away.

Our cows, Graceful and Gwen, were a consistent source of exasperation. Our cow expert, Charles Martell, made a very poignant observation when he said that if Graceful and Gwen decided to stop for the day, they would indeed stop for the day. He forgot to mention though that if they decided to go there was very little one could do to stop them: two cows bolting could

" TWO COWS BOLTING COULD NOT BE CALLED A STAMPEDE, BUT IT COULD FEEL LIKE ONE "

not be called a stampede but it could feel like one when you were next to them, holding on.

We gained a lot of satisfaction when the cows agreed to pull the harrows or plough, but it was always just that: an agreement by them to do some work. Peter and I persevered and eventually our cows seemed to actually respond to what we wanted, and even seemed to enjoy their labour. Their fitness levels also increased, which made it easier for them and us. They became more and more willing to be fitted with halters and yokes and, we liked to think, they understood their role within the farm – basically to pull heavy items that Peter and I could not. We certainly needed their raw power to get the big jobs done.

A winning combination – and I include myself in that! The raw power of cows would give any rugby scrum a challenge – a true pair of Tudor tractors

The sheep is a curious animal. Their complete lack of aggression means that one never feels apprehension when working with them but, though docile most of the time, they were given to panic, which could be both a blessing and a curse. Panic can make any animal unpredictable and a flock of panicking sheep are actually more of a threat to themselves than to any humans in the vicinity.

Washing them was an adventure but once our routine was in place we were soon an effective team. Peter and I would get the sheep down to the water, I would then hold the sheep in the water and Ruth would proceed to wash the sheep. Surprisingly, the sheep seemed to calm down once in the water: they do not like someone pouring water on them but when submersed they seemed more than happy. It is hard to dislike sheep but ours seemed to lack personality compared to the more characterful animals.

GEESE
The category of animals I would only work with out of necessity had a sole member: the geese. It is hard to find anything positive to say about them. Aesthetically the goose is a lovely looking bird, but personality-wise, they are extremely unpleasant.

A rare tranquil moment with one of our geese

Sparky, the fourth musketeer, once again steals the limelight!

Although we were delighted that some of our geese were sitting (on their eggs to protect them), it did mean that the whole gaggle was extremely unfriendly – more so than usual – and frequently stuck out their tongues, bared their teeth and hissed. It was quite easy to believe that birds were descended from dinosaurs at times. That was especially when two made a move for me from the front. While my concentration was definitely focused forward, another one circled around behind me and in a move of remarkable athleticism, jumped up, and simultaneously kicked me up the backside and bit me!

That action pretty much summed up my farm career with the geese. There was some light relief as we watched them waddle down the road to market, but any affection for them was short-lived. They were the bane of my time on the farm, always willing to attack and rarely providing any light relief (except at someone else's expense).

FINAL THOUGHTS

I think the most pertinent point of working with all these animals is the difference between working animals and pets. One can have affection for a working animal but one must understand that they need to be worked, and more importantly that, on the whole, they want to be.

The bond you make with farm animals is different to that with a household pet; affection plays its part but there is also a reliance on them to share the workload. You are in partnership with your animals and that develops respect for what they can do. Our farm experience confirmed the importance of these animals to the Tudors not as pets, but as workers and items of commerce. A farm in the Tudor period needed animals to work and eventually to make money. The secret for us seemed to be the diversity of our livestock; each animal or bird on the farm was not only a colourful character, but the key to its success.

THE COWS

Monarchs come and go, empires rise and fall but through it all country folk have taken up their ploughs and their harrows, their sickles and their scythes and grown crops to feed us all. In order to get a good crop the land has to be worked. This involves ploughing to turn over the existing vegetation and harrowing to break up the soil and work it into a fine 'tilth' (when the soil becomes like granulated coffee with a lot of air in it).

Gwen contemplating another hard day's work on the farm

When one thinks of ploughing with animals, it is often horses that come to mind. However, the horses' heyday was a short-lived affair that happened to coincide with the development of photographic technology. It was the development of the horse collar that allowed horses to be utilised as a draught animal because they pull from their chests. Prior to this, oxen were used extensively for fieldwork on farms for thousands of years (and still are in many parts of the world).

Oxen are castrated male cattle. A prize bull would be selected from birth and singled out for breeding, with the remaining males castrated to keep the animals docile while they are reared. These oxen can be broken for work and used on a farm up until the day that they go to the fattening pen and get slaughtered for their meat.

❝ TWO OXEN WHO ARE PAIRED UP WILL WORK TOGETHER FOR THE REST OF THEIR LIVES ❞

Graceful and Gwen, pictured in the 'wrong order'

Oxen pull from their shoulders and always work in pairs. The two oxen who are paired up will work together for the rest of their lives and they always have to be in the correct order. In the South Downs oxen were still being used up until the early 20th century; however, due to lack of demand and recent problems with TB there are now very few, if any, ploughing pairs left in the UK.

On our farm we had a couple of cows who had been broken for work in the past, but had spent the last two years being left idle. Never one to shy away from a challenge, we decided that they would become our farm's secret weapon.

In our area of the South Downs, the tradition is to name the ox on the left with a single syllable name and the ox on the right with a double syllable name, and in that tradition we decided to call ours Gwen and Graceful. They looked like something out of *Star Wars* as they emerged from the mist – and they were to be the power behind our rural idyll.

THE KIT

Stacked in a barn and getting covered in cobwebs was all the equipment we would need. There was a cart that would be handy for transporting goods, a roller for flattening the ground after sowing, to keep the birds off of our seeds, and a wooden harrows. The harrows would break up our soil with tines that could be knocked through as and when they broke or wore out. And, most importantly, there was a plough.

The plough was a replica of one used by the Romans in Britain, and had a very clever, reversible design. The coulter (cutting knife) can be angled using a hazel stick and the mould board (the board that turns the soil) can be taken off and reattached on the opposite side. Ours was, however, half the size it should have been, because while ploughing with oxen was traditionally done in teams of eight oxen, we had just two cows. Because our land was on chalk, the soil was fairly light, but had we been on heavy clay we would have needed at least a couple of extra cows.

In another thatched store we found all the tack we would need. There were a series of yokes of different sizes that had been made for our cows as they had grown up. The yoke sits on the shoulders of the cows and is fastened to each cow's neck through the use of a bent hazel rod, known as an oxbow. This is where the term oxbow lake comes from. The bows are held in place

Double-syllable Pe-ter on the right and single syllable Tom on the left

Making friends starts with a sniff

with pins and leather washers. In the middle of the yoke is a fastening point to which the kit can be fixed either directly in the case of the cart or by a chain or rope in the case of the harrows.

GETTING STARTED

Not only had our terrible twosome failed to work for a couple of years, they had also spent the best part of six months cooped up in a tiny area, being fed hay as the grass grew back. It took us a while but with a bit of gentle persuasion we managed to catch our cows and put them on the halter (a rope harness for their heads). Since they were so out of practice, we spent the first few days just establishing a routine and getting them used to the sound of our voices, our smell and our touch. Working with animals is very much a partnership.

But we already knew we were out of our depth – we had no idea what commands the cows had been broken to, so couldn't begin to start training them to plough. So we called in a man who had worked with them, and who has spent much of his life working with cattle: Charles Martell.

Watching Charles at work was something to behold. His movements were deliberate but subdued, and we could hear him set up a dialogue with the animal – a murmuring of soothing and encouraging words, punctuated with commands. Pretty soon the two cows were standing together, Gwen on the left, Graceful on the right, tethered to the posts ready to be yoked up.

To yoke the oxen, we placed the bows on the necks of the animals upside down, then the yoke is rested across them. It was key to keep the strongest animal (Graceful in our case) on a short leash and the weaker animal

> **" WE SPENT THE FIRST FEW DAYS ESTABLISHING A ROUTINE AND GETTING THEM USED TO THE SOUND OF OUR VOICES, OUR SMELL AND OUR TOUCH "**

(Gwen) on a longer one as she was easier to move over. The bows are then turned around and attached to the yoke with the fastenings on the inside holes in the middle, so that they can be reached from either side.

The next step was to find a goad – usually a piece of hazel. This is where the word hassle comes from, as it is used to literally hassle the oxen. Now for the science bit! When ploughing with a team of oxen a perch, rod or pole is used as a goad. A perch, rod or pole is a unit of measurement

Walking our cows up to work in the soon-to-be pea field

and is normally 5.5 yards in length. This was long enough to allow the ploughman to reach the front oxen, even from his position behind them, guiding the plough. As we only had two cows, we only needed a short goad.

Multiplying the length of the goad by 4 is 22 yards, which is the same length as a chain (or indeed a cricket wicket); multiplying by 40 is 220 yards, or is a furlong (the length an ox team could plough without a break). One chain multiplied by one furlong is equal to one acre – the amount of land an ox team could plough in a day.

When we got started, remarkably our cows remembered the commands they had been broken to. 'Walk on' got them started, 'back' put them in

" THE ONLY PROBLEM WAS THEY DIDN'T SEEM TO HAVE A COMMAND TO STOP! "

reverse, 'gee-away' turned them to the right and 'come-haw' turned them to the left. The only problem was they didn't seem to have a command to stop! We'd shout 'whoa' or 'stand' and use the goad as a barrier across their noses. As they built up a head of steam, we also used an emphatic use of the word 'steady' to take the edge off of their momentum.

One key element of the commands is to be loud. The oxen have better things on their minds like grazing and sleeping, so you need to get through to them. Charles said it has been known for oxen to fall asleep midway through ploughing.

We had to muzzle Gwen and Graceful so they would avoid the temptation of eating the grass

He also explained that when they have been doing a lot of work, oxen will accept almost any noise as a command to stop. There are accounts of oxen halting on the sound of the cowman breaking wind a little too loudly!

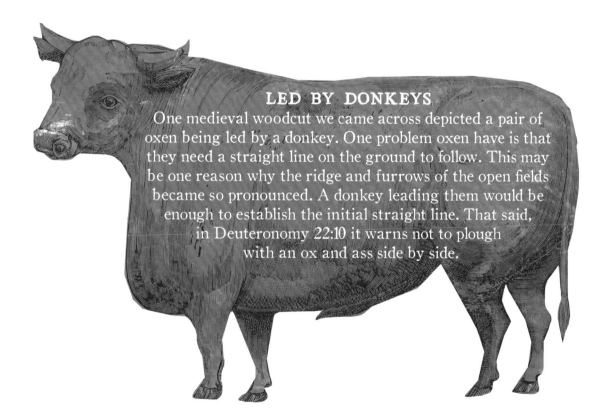

LED BY DONKEYS
One medieval woodcut we came across depicted a pair of oxen being led by a donkey. One problem oxen have is that they need a straight line on the ground to follow. This may be one reason why the ridge and furrows of the open fields became so pronounced. A donkey leading them would be enough to establish the initial straight line. That said, in Deuteronomy 22:10 it warns not to plough with an ox and ass side by side.

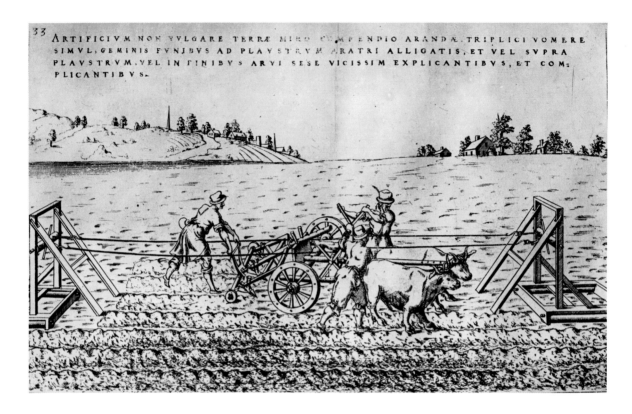

ARTIFICIVM NON VVLGARE TERRÆ MIRO COMPENDIO ARANDÆ, TRIPLICI VOMERE
SIMVL, GEMINIS FVNIBVS AD PLAVSTRVM ARATRI ALLIGATIS, ET VEL SVPRA
PLAVSTRVM, VEL IN FINIBVS ARVI SESE VICISSIM EXPLICANTIBVS, ET COM:
PLICANTIBVS.

It's pretty hard to plough with a cow in a straight line!

OUT IN THE FIELDS

We had them harnessed and we had the commands... now it was time to get them out in the fields. The time for excuses was over. The fact Gwen and Graceful hadn't seen grass or stretched their legs for so long meant they were, by nature, very flighty. However, on our ploughing day they behaved themselves, and soon enough we had them pulling the harrows and wrestling with the plough.

" WHILE WE DIDN'T HAVE ANY RUNAWAY MOMENTS, WE CERTAINLY CAME CLOSE "

The problem with oxen is that when they decide to go, there is little you can do to stop them. With a horse you have a bit in its mouth to give you an element of control, but no such luxury with your team of oxen. I found the goad to be useful, and while we didn't have any runaway moments, we certainly came close.

However, one of the problems ploughing with horses is that if the plough chain gets between their legs they often begin to panic and dance around. One of the benefits of using oxen is that they generally don't care: if they do have a bit of an episode and get tangled up in their harness, the best course of action is to leave them be and go and have a cup of tea. Charles said he has seen oxen with their yokes on upside down and back to front, but once they are settled again they are as placid as you like.

We had to get Gwen and Graceful's fitness levels up, which meant working them regularly. As they didn't have shoes we had to be careful where and how we worked them, especially as our ground was quite flinty. Shoeing an ox is quite a sight: while horses will stand patiently on three legs, oxen won't. To shoe an ox, they have to be lassoed and pulled to the ground. One person then sits on their neck, allowing the farrier to attach the shoes to each hoof. There are four pairs of shoes in total – two shoes for each cloven hoof. They often turn up in the archaeological record when a farmer ploughs his field looking like a broken horseshoe. Such finds are a testament to the animals that were the champions of fieldwork prior to the enclosure act of 1801 – the animals that were the engine of farming in Britain for millennia.

Man and beast (and Ruth) working in harmony

THE PIGS

PETER

 One of the most important animals in Tudor England was the pig. They were not only a source of meat, but an important trading commodity. Every part of the animal could be used including making glue from the bones and paintbrushes from the bristles. What's more, they were one of the most efficient waste disposal systems available to the Tudors. So with all that at stake, it was crucial that we took good care of our pigs and piglets if we were going to make our farm a success.

Tamworths have the intelligence of a Labrador and the escapology skills of Houdini

PIGGY EYED

The majority of pigs that are farmed today have been bred for their size so that they produce a lot of meat. They have been crossed with the Chinese breeds with characteristically floppy ears and this leads to the idea that they are blind (or at least short sighted). In reality their ears form a sight barrier but pigs have quite good eyesight.

Pigs are primarily a forest dwelling animal. They use their noses to dig out tasty treats such as brambles and bracken roots as they roam the woodland. This means that they are very good at breaking up soil and clearing the land. Pigs were often employed as a 'medieval rotavator' to prepare an area of overgrown land ready to take a crop: the term assarting refers to clearing forest land in preparation for cultivating an agricultural crop and pigs were vital to this process.

> **❝ PIGS WERE OFTEN EMPLOYED AS A 'MEDIEVAL ROTAVATOR' TO PREPARE AN AREA OF OVERGROWN LAND READY TO TAKE A CROP ❞**

Although not practised today, a pig could have its diet supplemented by human waste: kitchen scraps, and even our excrement. Unless we have chewed our food very well our bodies tend not to absorb all the nutrients from what we eat. By feeding our waste to the pigs, it is therefore possible to maximise that food.

Apart from wild boars (there are still a few wandering the English countryside today) the closest breed to a Tudor pig is the Tamworth. Tamworth pigs are a deep ginger colour and were described by Chaucer as being red like a fox. They have keen eyes and a good nature and are as intelligent as a labrador (which can have a grasp of around 1,000 words and commands).

It was around the 14th century that it became more common to build pigsties and keep a pig domestically rather than having them run free. One thing that monastic sites lack is evidence of pigsties but this does not mean they did not exist. To me, this implies that the pigs were moved as the land that they were kept on would become fertile and clear of vegetation, making it perfect to plant a crop with little fuss.

Top: Tom carries our ash
Middle: Peter checks the depth of the posthold
Bottom: The parallel bars will form our pigsties

FENCING THE AREA

We decided to build some pigsties to house a couple of Tamworths at our farm but first we had to pig-proof the area we wanted to contain them in. The idea of pig-proofing something is slightly misleading. If a pig wants to get out very little will stop it. Rather, we had to try and persuade the pigs to stay in.

To the south we built a dead hedge using the brush that we found lying around in the woods (particularly blackthorn) and we packed it in tightly. A dead hedge is quite an easy way to lay a hedge and if done well forms quite a good, solid barrier.

On the other three sides of our pig area, we constructed a wattle fence. We used sweet chestnut posts as they would last longer in the ground and wove between them hazel rods. The posts have to be spaced according to the thickness of the rods: as our rods were fairly stout we spaced our posts one and a half feet apart. We then worked in the hazel poles keeping all the butt ends on one side. We alternated the weave by putting one butt up against a sweet chestnut post, weaved that in, put the next butt up against the next post, weaved that in and so on. As long as the poles weave between four posts, then the weave will be strong.

When we got to the end we would turn around and come back. Unless the fence is circular, the ends have fewer poles therefore they tend to drop off in height. To compensate we added a few extra poles to bulk them up a bit. The wattle fence once finished looked fantastic: it was very strong and provided a sight barrier for the pigs, convincing them to stay in their area. All the pigs needed now was a shelter.

THE PIGSTIES

Pigs can deal with pretty much anything but equally, they do like their creature comforts. One thing that pigs aren't overly fond of is a draught. We decided to make the best sties we possibly could that were dry, solid, could take a pig scratching against them and were draught free.

Wattle and daub butting up to an ash pole

To make our pigsties we used only materials sourced from the landscape we were in: timber from the forest, wood from the coppice, clay from the ground, and straw and dung from the farm. We decided on a timber frame building with a shingle roof and wattle and daub walls. This is very much in the style of medieval buildings, though it was only really at the Tudor period that these buildings became fixed in the landscape. In the early medieval period, there was a tendency for settlement shift (due to external forces). Entire villages would migrate as time progressed, meaning that people would have been used to constructing buildings quite swiftly.

> ❝ ENTIRE VILLAGES WOULD MIGRATE AS TIME PROGRESSED, MEANING THAT PEOPLE WOULD HAVE BEEN USED TO CONSTRUCTING BUILDINGS QUITE SWIFTLY ❞

We started out by digging eight postholes. They were about one foot deep and only penetrated the subsoil: given soil creep and ploughing, it is unlikely that these would show up in the archaeological record. For our upright posts we felled some ash trees as there was an abundance of them, having self-seeded over the years. Ash makes great furniture and has a good straight grain but it doesn't do too well outside. However, these sties were only temporary and the wood would be covered. We packed in our uprights using flints and we cut various mortise, tenon and bird mouth joints and pegged the frame together. We then drilled holes for our rods ready for our wattle.

WATTLE AND DAUB

If you go to a builders' merchants with an idea of partitioning a room, the chances are that you will buy studwork timber and plasterboard. This is essentially what wattle and daub has become. Wattle is the name given to the weave of sticks (usually hazel) onto which daub (a mixture of clay, straw and cow dung) is squished. This became plaster and lathe (thin wooden strips), which in turn became plasterboard. There is one major difference between plasterboard and wattle and daub, however, and that is the strength of the latter.

Wattling up to the top of the pigsties

We wove our hazel wands (one or two years growth, about the size of your little finger) between our rods (four or five years growth, about the size of your thumb). These were spaced around 10–15 cm apart and the whole structure became more solid.

The wattle not only forms a wall upon which to slap the daub but it also locks everything together. It is also quite surprising how quickly you can wattle when you get a rhythm going. The key is to try and always bend the wands equally as you weave them, otherwise they might fracture. As they go round a corner, you need to twist them to break the fibres up and stop them snapping (like making thatching spars).

The wattle has to be woven on when it is green so it can bend. In my opinion, when the daub goes on it preserves the wattle and stops (or at least slows) it drying out and going brittle. The daub is a mix of clay for substance, cow dung for elasticity and straw as a binding agent. The daub goes on both sides of the wattle and as it is pushed into the gaps, the two layers of daub meet and compress together. It is very solid: although it will crack as it dries, the straw stops it falling off. If you wanted to, you could skim the daub with some lime plaster to give that classic Tudor look (we didn't, as these were 'just' pigsties).

> **" THE PIG IS BY FAR THE MOST DANGEROUS ANIMAL ON THE FARM: IF THEY TURN ON YOU, THEY CAN KILL YOU "**

The daub is slapped on in 'cats' – a term that may derive from the tradition of putting kittens in the foundations to ward off mice. It is cold and gritty and can be tough on the hands if done in the winter months. The finish, though, is well worth it. If the building were to burn down the fire would harden the clay in the daub and lumps of this show up in the archaeological record. They are smooth on one side and lumpy on the other, often with perfect impressions of wattle wands in them.

SHINGLES

Once our walls were up, we had to put a roof on. The pitch of our roof was too shallow for thatch and even if it had been okay, we didn't have access to any decent thatching material anyway. Instead, we opted to make wooden shingles. A shingle (or shake) is essentially a tile made from split wood, usually oak or cedar. They are usually 18 inches in length and are laid exactly the same as tiles.

The key to getting a good shingle is access to straight-grained wood with relatively few knots. We had a couple of large rounds of wood and using a froe (a long flat cutting blade attached to a long handle) we started eking out our shingles. It was hard work at first but soon we had our eye in and could read the wood, seeing where the next split should be made. It was surprising just how many shingles we could get out of a large log. We laid our shingles on hazel rods and pegged them in place overlapping the joints with the next row of shingles. As roofs go it looked pretty tidy but we didn't have long to marvel as soon our pigs turned up.

Top: All they need now is a shingle roof
Bottom: Mother and babies happy inside

THE PIGS ARRIVE

We took delivery of two Tamworth sows named Georgie and Mildred, each with three piglets. To get them in we couldn't herd them (pigs don't herd very well), so instead we had to persuade them by throwing bread. These pigs had been used to roaming open woodland and it was quite a test to see how they took to our little area.

They were also as close to wild as one can get. The pig is by far the most dangerous animal on the farm: if they turn on you, they can kill you. However, we struck up quite a good friendship with ours, spending a lot of time dispensing much-needed scratches and making sure they had mud baths to protect their sensitive skin from the sun.

It soon came the time to wean the young ones and put the boar in. I always find weaning quite heart wrenching as the youngsters cry for their mums but it had to be done. We put the little ones up in the forest. In Tudor times (and earlier) this was known as the right to pannage. It was a common right to release your pigs into the woodlands at a set time of the year to feed off of the fallen acorns. Pannage is not practised much these days but still persists in the New Forest.

Tom's Diary

THE PIGSTY

Making our Tudor pigsty was our first main project, and one we thought would be good practice for the hands-on, practical style of farming that we'd need to get to grips with. At the start we were not feeling the pressure so, while sitting in a field in the sun, we created a 3D plan of what the pigsty should look like out of twigs and leaves, discussing such factors as wind direction and materials.

At this stage we were happy and convinced that knocking up a pigsty would a great start to our Tudor farm experience. Building a structure with unworked timber will always challenge the most positive people. Luckily, Peter and I have known each other for years and a

combination of our good working relationship, my pragmatism and
Peter's patience meant that when my urge to hit things with an axe or
mallet was growing strong, Peter was able to step in with a cool eye
and appraise what had vexed me. Likewise, before Peter could suggest
adding all the mod-cons for our pigs, I could bring him to heel.

The building effort was, in effect, 'Tudor Tetris'. The wood we picked
was as straight as we could find but when trying to build a timber
box it soon became evident how un-straight it was! And when daubing
I discovered that, regardless of how hard you try, you will get dirty!
It didn't take long to cover a large area, but the secret is consistency
of application: if your daub is too thickly applied, then the weight will
pull the daub off the wattle; if your application is too thin the daub
will become very brittle when it dries and will probably crack. The
changeable British weather was a constant threat to our daubing as
well. One day the rain would soak it; the next the sun would bake it,
meaning the daub went from one extreme to the other regularly.

It was the roof, and the effort required to make the shingles (wood
roof tiles) that brought us the most stress: we needed every ounce of
endurance and brute force to break up our huge stumps of elm tree into
rectangular wooden miniature planks. The finished project, however,
looked amazing, a little like a wooden Giant's Causeway. Pleasingly,
not only did the pigs love it, but it withstood the machinations of these
ever curious creatures!

THE SHEEP

To be a Tudor farmer, especially on monastic land, the chances were you had sheep. In the period we were looking at there was a lot of money in sheep farming. This wasn't from their meat: that started slightly later as land became enclosed, breeding patterns changed and a market demand was created by an increasing population and expanding towns. Instead, it was all related to the wool trade, and therefore sheep shearing. So shearing must have been a big event as it was the time of year when you earned your money.

Sheep at market prior to being sheared

I have been left with an unwelcome memento of shearing from a previous agricultural adventure. Having sheared most of our sheep, we got up early the next morning and headed up the hill to finish the job. Tired and bleary eyed, I wasn't concentrating. I cornered a sheep at the end of a lane and had hold of it, but it was up a bank so I let it go to then recapture it at ground level. It jumped down as planned... but one of its long staples of wool caught the end of my middle finger and snapped the bone in four places. When I made a fist with my left hand, my middle finger bent over the top of my ring and little finger. Ever since then I have always been wary of sheep, but with this project, there was to be no escape.

MOVING THE SHEEP

We had a paddock directly next to our farmhouse, which would have been a good place for a Tudor farmer to have kept them over winter, but during the rest of the year sheep were put out to pasture. This is known as transhumance and is often practised in mountainous or rugged areas such as Wales or Dartmoor. In our area, the sheep would most likely have been moved to common land on the downs. In the open field system, it makes

Get used to that hedge - soon you'll be enclosed!

sense for a village to have their farmland close by and the land where they put their animals farther away: a farmer would need to tend the fields more often than they would need to tend to their sheep.

> " A FARMER WOULD NEED TO TEND THE FIELDS MORE OFTEN THAN THEY WOULD NEED TO TEND TO THEIR SHEEP "

Rounding up and moving sheep is relatively easy... in theory. Moving sheep from highland to lowland and vice versa works well because the older sheep know what they are doing and where they are going. In order to move them, we armed ourselves with crooks for the woodland areas, but in large, open spaces, our secret weapon came into play – Bess, the bearded collie. Tudor sheep dogs were used differently from the sheep dogs of today like border collies. They were mainly used for driving the sheep. We used Bess as a flanker so we could push the sheep along the tree line.

Shearing and harvesting. A little Tudor poetic licence

WASHING TIME

When we finally got the sheep back to the farm the first job was to wash them. It is possible to wash a fleece after it is sheared but it was usually washed while still part of the sheep.

The fleece needs to be as clean as possible before the wool is sold as this aids the price. More importantly, all the detritus that a sheep's fleece picks up in its life needs to be washed out so it doesn't blunt the shears.

The majority of washing happened in a river. Often a barrier of stones or hurdles would be erected to bank up the water and the sheep would be washed one by one. You do need to be fairly careful as it is possible (though unlikely) to drown a sheep.

Once the sheep are washed they need to dry. This can take a while especially if the weather is not too great but luckily we had good sunshine. While they are drying it is also important to keep the sheep clean, so that they don't undo all your hard work.

TO CATCH A SHEEP

Before we could get started shearing, we had to catch a sheep. I maintain that catching sheep is some of the best rugby practice available. They can be pretty smart and can often read your body language. Once they make a break to get round you as you back them into a corner, that's when you have to make your move. I always mentally tell myself that I'm not going to be beaten by a sheep. Well, not twice at least.

> **" SHEEP CAN BE PRETTY SMART AND CAN OFTEN READ YOUR BODY LANGUAGE "**

Once you have the sheep by the wool, you pretty much have it under control. If you place a sheep sitting up or on its back as is done with modern shearing then that's when it goes all limp and soft. It is often thought that they die if the wool is not cut but in fact, they are more likely to get flystrike. Flystrike is where flies lay their eggs in the hot sweaty fleece: these turn into maggots and when the maggots grow mouths they start feeding on the

" IT IS OFTEN THOUGHT THAT THEY DIE IF THE WOOL IS NOT CUT BUT IN FACT, THEY ARE MORE LIKELY TO GET FLYSTRIKE "

sheep. It is this that can be fatal to sheep. As the maggots hatch, there is a chance the sheep will try to scratch their backs; this can also be fatal as if the sheep gets on its back it can't get up again, its body weight slowly crushing its organs.

The other way to control a sheep is by its head. Forefinger and thumb can be placed like a horse's bit in the sheep's mouth and the head can be turned towards the sky. The major danger when up close with a sheep is that it will twist and break your leg at the knee. You need to be very careful that you're in a position where this won't happen. It is very unlikely but every now and then you get tired and lose concentration.

Our flocks of sheep eating down the grass prior to shearing

MAKING A SHEARING BENCH

PETER

shearing bench is like a slatted ladder on legs that tapers to a seat at one end. As they are made of wood, very few survive, and the museums that own the few that do exist were reluctant to let me, Ruth and Tom use them to shear our rather large South Downs sheep. So instead, we had to make one from scratch.

I could have searched for the perfect tree with a fork or an S-shaped bow that could be split but in order to get the shape I wanted, I decided to steam some hazel as we had an abundance of it in our coppice. To do this I went into the woods and dug a square pit in the ground about six feet long, two feet deep and two feet wide. I lined the base with stones that I had collected and on top of these I built a fire. The idea was to store as much heat in the stones as I could. As the fire raged, I boiled up some water in a cauldron and surrounded the pit with wet straw to start heating it up. I then cut down two hazel poles and trimmed them to about five and a half feet in length. They were around two to three inches thick.

More than anything, it is fire that separates us from the animal kingdom

While this was going on, I began to prepare the slats and the legs for the bench. I also fashioned some stout pegs to stake in the ground around which I planned to bend my wood. When the time finally came I uncovered my hazel poles and gingerly picked them up. They were piping hot and I had to handle them quickly and carefully. I was amazed at how easily they bent round my stakes. Once in place I left them there to cool down and set in that shape.

A couple of days later I undid my ties and took my bent hazel from the stakes. At this point, it was a simple case of drilling some holes to put the slats and the legs in place and pegging the whole lot together. My only worry was whether it would hold the weight of a sheep. There was only one way to find out...

Green wood is very good for steaming and this is why I cut the poles as late as possible. I then raked out the large embers of the fire and smothered the others with my wet straw into which I encased my two hazel poles. I poured on my cauldron of water, which had now reached a rolling boil, and covered the whole lot with soil. The stones should act as a heat source and turn the water to steam. This in turn should be forced into the wood to soften the wood fibres. A good rule of thumb is you need an hour's worth of steaming for every inch of wood that needs to be bent so I would have to leave my steaming grave for a good three hours.

A finished and usable Tudor shearing bench

TOM

SHEARING

Peter's efforts with the shearing bench were well rewarded when we put it
into use. The bench was relatively easy to put together and sturdy enough
to take my weight (83 kg) and that of a sheep. Once it had been lashed
together with sisal there was no sway in the structure at all, ensuring that
we had a steady platform to work off.

Acting with our sheep-shearing expert, Ed, I was able to easily manipulate
the sheep onto the bench and take up my position at the top end, where the
steam-bent wood became narrower. Their fleeces can give the impression
that the sheep are much bigger than they actually are, but luckily the
thick fleece actually makes them easy to manoeuvre. Although I used the
bench in tandem with Ed to shear one sheep at a time (one person gently
controlling the sheep by holding the head), Ed was also able to shear a
sheep alone, lying a sheep across the width of the bench and trapping the
head under one arm. Considering these sheep were shearlings, meaning
they had never been sheared before, they were remarkably calm both with
the process and with lying on the bench – a situation that must have been
very alien for them.

The shearing process itself was
a matter of concentration and
maintaining a steady pace. The aim is
to cut as close to the skin as possible
and to cut just once: that way one
protects the sheep and maintains the
value of the fleece. The shape of the
sheep's body directly reflects how
easy that process is; over the expanse
of the belly and back, it is easy to pull
the skin taut with one's spare hand to
prevent the clippers catching a fold of
skin. Unfortunately, the areas where
the skin begins to sag, around the
legs for instance, is much trickier,
and when it is cut, should be covered
with sheep salve to prevent infection
or worse (see page 114). However,

*After shearing, this sheep was
inscrutable but surely happier
in the hot weather*

" THE SHEARING PROCESS ITSELF WAS A MATTER OF CONCENTRATION AND MAINTAINING A STEADY PACE "

apart from the one nick to a ewe on the inside of her leg, all the sheep had a clean bill of health after the shearing. The salve, too, fulfilled its purpose and the ewe soon healed with no evidence of infection or maggots!

As for myself, I really noticed the different muscles in my body working as I moved the sheep around: it felt like a good workout. Unfortunately, the position I had to adopt to do my shearing meant that a lot of pressure went through my lower back, prolonged by my shearing lesson from Ed.

By default, the importance of technique in Tudor times was emphasised: shepherds could be shearing hundreds of sheep over the period of a few weeks and to avoid any long-term damage they would have to get their position right and their speed up, so that they would not be hunched over the sheep for a prolonged period. An adherence to these principles potentially would allow them to work long hours without picking up any short-term or chronic injuries themselves.

The sheep look like peeled oranges when they are shorn. We were all for patting ourselves on the back when we had finished – but then we remembered we forgot to check the feet. And attempting to catch a sheep that no longer has any wool is like trying to pick up a wet bar of soap...

FEET

Checking the feet is of paramount importance. The nails that protect the hoof wear away naturally if the sheep is on rocky ground but if they are kept in soft pasture then the nails can grow over the feet and need to be cut off. We also needed to check that there were no stones, especially flints, stuck in their hooves and have a good look at their teeth. They all looked fine, although one of them was quite old, and then a few weeks later Ruth made us a fantastic spit roasted piece of mutton that had been basted and dredged to form a crust...

TOM

SALVE

Sheep salve was invaluable for maintaining the value of the flock, and the Tudors created a concoction from easily accessible ingredients that could be made on a regular basis. While the Tudor era was a period of relative stability after the ructions of the Wars of the Roses, the Tudor yeomen still had the pragmatic approach enforced by civil war when resources are sparse. There was very little waste, a huge amount of recycling and a reliance on what materials lay around that could be pressed into service. The salve itself was an easy job that could be done in between larger jobs. Once you had amassed your ingredients it did not take much more than an hour to make the mixture. Together with a steady fire, all the equipment I borrowed was from Ruth's kitchen (washing everything up afterwards to avoid a scolding).

I made the salve by chopping up broom (a mixture of leaves and flowers) and leaving it in a pan with rainwater. When the mixture became thick in consistency, I added two pounds of sheep suet and melted it over a gentle heat, while stirring. Then came the secret ingredient – brine, and a 'pottell of old piss'. This urine must be left for three weeks before introducing it to the mixture so that it can react with the oxygen and thus create ammonia. It is this ammonia that forms part of the sterilising component. This delightful concoction was then strained through some muslin and left to solidify – a process which takes several days. What I was left with was somewhere between a paste and a gel. Unassuming enough, but it was a crucial ingredient in the health of our flock, and a defence against flystrike – a problem which still affects flocks today.

A flock in fine health, if only medium spirits. Healthy sheep ensured healthy wool and meat products.

THE WOOL TRADE

If you talk to a modern hand-shearer, they will tell you their job is to get the job done as quickly as possible. There is still a pride in getting the wool off in one but the fleece has very little worth – or at least, not the value it had in the Tudor period. It was because of this value that the Tudor shearing method was different. Rather than trying to get the fleece off whole, Tudor farmers were more concerned with getting the best price for their wool and this meant that they sorted as they went. The best wool went in one basket, while that which was a bit straggly or needed more attention was placed in another.

Ruth spinning a great Tudor yarn

We took our wool off to be evaluated for sale by historian James Clark and wool assayer Richard Martin. Prior to the dissolution, the monasteries were entrenched in the wool trade. Wool was very expensive but there were a lot of people who needed to make a cut, so what a farmer was paid was not what the wool was worth. Furthermore, there was often a time lag in payment. In our case, it might be over a year before we see any money from the transaction.

> **" FARMERS STILL HAD TO PRODUCE THE BEST WOOL POSSIBLE AND MONASTERIES WOULD OVERLOOK A FARMER WHOSE WOOL DIDN'T COME UP TO SCRATCH "**

As tenant farmers, we would not be selling our wool directly to the cloth merchants. Instead we would be selling it through the monastery. Monasteries were like brands: merchants knew that if they went to a certain monastery they would get a certain quality. In order to maintain this quality, the wool that the monastery sold each year was a blend of wools, a bit like instant coffee or blended whisky. If the monastery only sold the best wool then they wouldn't be able to maintain the standard or the volume year on year. This didn't mean that the monasteries would take any old rubbish. Farmers still had to produce the best wool possible and monasteries would overlook a farmer whose wool didn't come up to scratch.

Richard showed us what to look for when evaluating the wool. Factors to note are the colour (it needs to be all white for the cloth trade), if there is any vegetable matter in with the wool, how long the staple is and if the shearer has done a double cut (this is when the shears cut the wool twice and basically chop it up). Picking the wool up, you can feel the size of it; if you wrap it into a strand and pull it apart, it should snap with a ping rather than tear and pull apart. The sheep's diet directly affects the growth of the wool, so the better the diet the better the wool. This is mainly a problem in winter.

The wool trade at the time was essentially a futures market and prices did fluctuate year on year. This meant that it was possible to hold back wool in the hope that the price would rise the next year. The danger was that storing wool was a risky business. It will go off and there are fungi that can grow. All in all, it was like farming any product. You had to work your hardest and do your best. Even then, you were not guaranteed to make money.

The quality of the thread that makes the cloth is directly related to the ability and efforts of the farmer

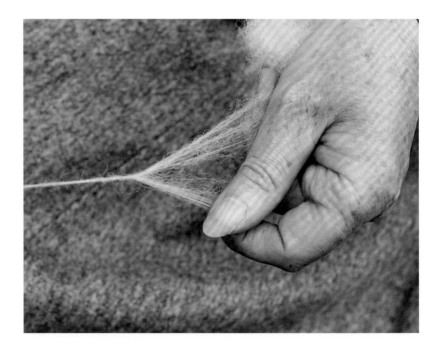

SHEPHERDING AND CROOK MAKING

Shepherding in Tudor times was the epitome of teamwork and ingenuity. Whether it was a lone shepherd working with a pair of dogs or a team of shepherds working with crooks, they would need to manoeuvre their flocks over fields, down lanes and through forests. I have talked already about our working dog, Bess, and how well she worked with our flock, but there was another way to manipulate our easily confused sheep into doing what we wanted: the shepherd's crook.

A traditional 16th-century woodcut showing shepherds at work

The crook was a stick with a cow horn attached to one end, that would be filled with pebbles. It was a kind of handheld catapult similar to a lacrosse stick that allowed the shepherd to control the flock from a distance, using missiles to startle the sheep into doing what was wanted. At no stage should the actual crook come into contact with the sheep. Three shepherds would position themselves behind the flock but taking responsibility for different areas around the flock; for instance, the shepherd on the left would watch the left flank of the flock and make sure they did not make a break to the left by throwing pebbles out in front of the scampering sheep (and the same with the right-hand shepherd). The middle shepherd had arguably the trickiest job as he or she would be responsible for making sure the sheep did not bolt out ahead.

The premise plays upon the shy, insecure sheep reacting to the sound of the stones or mud hitting the undergrowth or the sight of stones cartwheeling across a field in front of them or to the sides. The sheep then alter course to avoid further missiles that might land in the same area. Obviously this requires some co-operation from the sheep and calm shepherds with steady hands; otherwise, the size of one's flock could be drastically reduced as wayward stones concuss sheep left, right and centre. The action is easiest if one uses one hand as a pivot point and other hand to swing down the unloaded end of the crook, bringing up the loaded end like a catapult. The technique is less labour-intensive for the shepherd by using physics to do the work. A wise shepherd would load up with pebbles before setting off on a trek, though the capability of these tools was not reduced by using mud if it was moist: it would be just as loud in a wooded area. It is unlikely, though, that if the crook was employed as an offensive weapon that mud would have as much effect as stones against a rabid dog.

Controlling sheep with a crook is another example of the Tudors finding ways to be efficient and inventive. At a time when metalwork was becoming more and more common, the Tudor shepherd was still being pragmatic, using his or her surroundings to find materials to make an extremely simple but effective tool. The shepherds were hardy folk, spending an extensive amount of time outdoors in the elements and facing threats to their sheep from the elements, wildlife and humans. If the shepherds did not work with dogs, then having a crook was vital.

Sometimes a sheep's blatant distrust of humans was enough to encourage them to move off in any direction one wanted. They always knew where the gate was...

MAKING A CROOK

Cow horn cut to form a crook similar to a catapult for small missiles and mud

* The crook, as simple as it is, can be made from items foraged from the countryside. It requires few tools and does not take long to make:
* Take a straight hazel rod and a cow horn.
* Cut the hazel to a workable length. Dependent on the height of person using the crook, four to five foot should work for most people.
* Strip the bark from the rod using an axe, knife or billhook. This is not strictly necessary but as the shaft will be moving through the hands repeatedly, then it will make it more comfortable to use. Aesthetically, it looks better too.
* Take the cow horn and starting from the tip, estimate a distance to cut so that one can slide the horn onto one's hazel rod snugly.
* Using a small hand-saw, cut twice from the other end of the horn – one vertical cut, one horizontal cut – so that a right-angled section can be removed.
* Fit the cut horn onto the hazel rod, securing with a nail if necessary.

❝ CONTROLLING SHEEP WITH A CROOK IS ANOTHER EXAMPLE OF THE TUDORS FINDING WAYS TO BE EFFICIENT AND INVENTIVE ❞

SHEEPISH SPORTS

Crooks were not only a useful shepherding tool, but the technique of skilfully flinging clods of earth and pebbles to change your sheep's course could well have been the inspiration behind games such as shinty, hurling and lacrosse.

THE GEESE

PETER

I t is thought that the goose was domesticated in ancient Egypt, probably based upon the bas-relief that depicts the force-feeding of the animal (and implying that the Egyptians also knew about the delicacy foie gras). Geese were also an important animal in the Roman Empire and were dedicated to the goddess Juno. The Roman author and naturalist Pliny the Elder documented the goose march from northern Gaul to Rome in his encyclopaedia *Natural History* (AD 77–79): in Britain, likewise, geese would have been marched from farms to markets.

Taking my goose to market (or is it my goose taking me to market?)

Traditionally, goose is eaten at the feast of Michaelmas on 29th September each year: this accounts for the original date of Nottingham Goose Fair, which up until 1752 was held on 21st September. The other fair to carry a reference to geese in the UK is Goosey Fair in Tavistock, which is believed to have its origins in a 12th-century Michaelmas fair. The feast of Michaelmas represents the end of the harvest and the descent into winter and shorter days. There was a belief that if you held up the breast bone of your goose that you had just eaten to the light, the darker it was the harsher the winter was going to be.

❝ GEESE PROVIDE MEAT, EGGS AND FEATHERS THAT CAN BE USED FOR A VARIETY OF PURPOSES ❞

Geese provide meat, eggs and feathers that can be used for a variety of purposes. Under the rules set by the Benedictine monasteries the consumption of eggs and fresh birds was not prohibited, leading to quite a demand. From the 13th century onwards there is evidence of monasteries rearing geese, hens and ducks. Huge amounts of eggs were also being brought into the monastery implying that surrounding farms would have stocked poultry as well. Furthermore, goose houses are found in the surviving records of certain monasteries: Durham Priory had a goose house paved with flagstones, demonstrating that they were more than just a passing fad.

As geese were driven to market over such long distances, their feet were protected with the use of tar or sacking. We really wanted to give tar a go as I have often read about it but never seen it done. Instead, though, we went with sacking: we fashioned small booties for each of our geese and one by one grabbed them and attached their new footwear. I was expecting them to straight away be worrying their new additions but they didn't seem to mind wearing shoes.

I still think that geese make one of the tastiest dishes but during the reign of Henry VIII, turkeys were introduced to the UK. This gave rise to competition as the Victorian goose as the Christmas dish. Coupled with the declining celebration for feast of Michaelmas and changes in farming practices, the numbers of geese in the UK has reduced rapidly ever since.

Our geese off to forage for food

HOME AND GARDEN

The home and garden is the nucleus of the farm. Everything goes on around it but ultimately it is all to keep the home fires burning. It is from the home that we get our daily bread, where we rest our head and where we treat and recover from any ailments we may have. It is in the home that a Tudor farmer could display their wealth or success and where they could retreat from public life.

So much of what goes on in the home is dictated by the garden. As plants come into season the diet changes and it is here in the garden where medicines are grown. It is a barometer for the farm: if the garden is flourishing, then the crops should be doing well but if it had been a bad year and the garden is in a poor state then the fields may not be faring much better. Any Tudor farmer worth their salt knew that to impress and to run a good farm, they first needed to get their home and garden in order.

KEEPING HOUSE

Cleanliness was much prized in early Tudor Britain. No one had heard of germs, bacteria or viruses but the unpleasantness of dirt was apparent to all. Bad smells were believed to be carriers of infection and disease and anyone with hopes of a healthy life did their best to avoid or eradicate them. The corruption of foodstuffs quite clearly rendered them unfit for consumption, with even the smallest speck of rot or decay quickly spreading among stored edible goods.

Achieving cleanliness was largely a matter of hard work and a small number of useful ingredients. Potash, ammonia, acetic acid and salt provided the main chemical elements of the armoury against dirt, while sand, chalk, soot, fuller's earth, and brick dust provided support. Further assistance came from the herb garden in the form of mare's tail, tansy, wormwood, soapwort, rosemary, sage and thyme.

Scouring with sand

*Sand, grass and
rosemary constitute
a washing-up kit*

POTASH

Potash was derived from wood ash. It could be used directly to help clean
greasy pots or in a cleaner, more concentrated form called lye. It was made
using the bottom of an old tub or barrel, which was pierced repeatedly.
A layer of clean small stones or gravel an inch or two thick was put into
the bottom, then a little clean sand went on top followed by three or four
inches of clean straw to form a filter. Wood ash from the fire was added to
the tub over several days until a good thick layer had built up.

❝ COLLECTED IN A SEPARATE VESSEL, URINE WILL FERMENT CHANGING TO AMMONIA IN AROUND THREE VERY SMELLY, WEEKS ❞

The tub was then raised up over a smaller one and water was slowly poured
in the top. As the water trickled down, it picked up the chemicals from the
ash, with the gritty bits being filtered out and the pure lye dripping into
the tub underneath. For a really concentrated lye, the first batch could be

ABRASIVES
The 'mechanical' ingredients, the sand, chalk,
fuller's earth, soot and so on, all helped increase the
efficiency of scrubbing. Aided by these abrasives it
was possible to get into all the nooks and crannies
and to shift dirt from any surface.

run through several times. Alternatively, you could boil up the liquid lye, driving off steam and leaving the more concentrated solution behind. The lye that resulted was highly alkali in nature (that's why it was called lye). It dissolved grease and, by altering the pH balance, killed bacteria.

AMMONIA AND OTHER AIDS

Ammonia was derived from urine. Collected in a separate vessel, urine will ferment, changing to ammonia in around three, very smelly, weeks. Unsurprisingly, most people kept their ammonia pots firmly lidded and outside the house.

Wood ash scrubbed around with a handful of grass or straw cleans even the greasiest of frying pans with ease

Ammonia is an excellent bleach, both for whitening stains and killing bacteria. Acetic acid came from vinegar or alegar (the 'vin' and 'ale' parts of the word denoting whence it was derived, the 'gar' part of the word meaning alcohol that had turned sour). It is an excellent de-scaling agent, a mild dissolver of grease and an anti-bacterial agent. Salt, meanwhile, unsurprisingly also kills bacteria; it is after all a major form of food preservation.

Most of the herbs acted as insecticides, driving out fleas, ants and lice from the home. Soapwort however, as the name implies, has a sap that acts rather like a mild soap and mare's tail contains a very high silica content which makes it into a natural scouring pad.

Soap itself was something of a rarity: it was produced by taking lye and boiling it up with lots of animal fat and a sprinkle of salt. The fat was in short supply, being required for eating and cooking first and foremost, but also to make rushlights, to grease the axles of carts, to make medicines, aid the spinning of wool and a host of other functions. Most people saw no reason to make soap, when the lye itself did the job.

A splash of vinegar is ideal for washing up crockery and wooden utensils

DOING THE WASHING UP

The very greasiest of pans can be cleaned simply with the warmth of a dying fire, a handful of wood ash, a bunch of straw and a rinse of cold water. Wood ash, containing the chemicals that form lye, dissolves grease all by itself. If the pan is still warm, a little wood ash rubbed around with a handful of disposable straw will lift the grease and scrub any burnt-on bits. When done, the ashy straw can be discarded, back into the fire. A splash of rinsing water takes away any stray bits of straw and ash.

Stubborn burnt-on food can be removed with sand or mare's tail. Mare's tail, if you have it, is in itself a disposable scourer, needing nothing but a splash of water. Scrunch the plant up in your hand and scrub, throwing it away when it becomes dirty. If you don't have any mare's tail handy then take a damp rag and dip it into a bowl of sand: a layer of sand will adhere to the cloth and this forms your scouring pad. The sand can then be simply rinsed away once it has done its job.

Platters, cups and bowls rarely need such harsh action, nor should you inflict it upon them too often as it will wear them away. Turn instead to a splash of vinegar in hot water, a clean rag or a handful of rosemary to wash them with. Knives (they are not stainless steel, so rusting is an issue) are best cleaned with a paste of chalk and water and dried immediately. This type of paste is what most modern 'kitchen cleaner' products are based upon.

CLOTHES

RUTH

The clothes worn by monks and nuns seem very specific to us: they are uniforms that go with the lifestyle, religious dress unrelated to the wear of the rest of society. But at their inception, the garments worn within the monastery were nothing more than a conservative version of everyday clothing.

In renouncing the world, members of the community were giving up vanity and social display. As each order was founded and the rule written, the clothes that they determined on were respectable, unfussy, practical and unremarkable. If such a foundation began today we would probably have to imagine the religious dress as being an old-fashioned cut of jeans, plain T-shirt and a long-sleeved, plain brown or blue jumper.

By 1500, the religious foundations had been in existence for several hundred years and their clothing was archaic and symbolic, much as it seems to be today. Men's fashion had changed much more dramatically than that of women, so monks were very much more distinctive from laymen than nuns were from laywomen. Women still wore floor length garments, albeit much more fitted at the waist than those of nuns. Men had turned their backs on long tunics, favouring fitted leg hose and short coats instead – a radically different silhouette.

> **" SOME MONKS AND NUNS APPEAR TO HAVE ENJOYED EXTENSIVE WARDROBES WHILST OTHERS WORE NOTHING BUT THE MOST BASIC OF GARMENTS "**

The clothes of monks and nuns may have been distinctive, but were not always, or even usually produced or issued communally. Many monks and nuns provided their own clothing, albeit to the general cut and colour of their chosen institution. As a result, the quality and the detail of the clothing could be quite varied between individuals in the same house. Records speak of habits in an array of different types of wool, and in a variety of qualities, thickness and finishes. They also mention additional types of garment, such as cloaks, that do not appear among the clothing

Whilst laywomen and nuns still had elements of dress in common, laymen and monks dressed very differently

rules of the order. Some monks and nuns appear to have enjoyed extensive wardrobes whilst others wore nothing but the most basic of garments. Several houses record the practice of giving out a regular cash sum to monks for them to purchase their own clothing, though entry requirements often stipulated that the novice is to bring a full set with them.

WHAT MONKS WORE

Our landlords, the Benedictine order of monks, wore black habits. Their basic garment was a floor length tunic, belted at the waist. Over this they could wear a scapular for working in. This was envisaged as an apron and consisted of a long straight piece of shoulder width fabric that went over the head and reached down below the knees front and back. If the monk was engaged in ceremonial duties, such as the choir, he was to wear his hood. The hoods of English Benedictines were well known for their long length, with the tip hanging down to the backs of their knees when they uncovered their heads. In cold weather they also wore a cowl or over-gown.

All of these garments were woollen. Linen underwear, in the form of shirts, were not part of the rule, but their occasional appearance in the

Peter in his doublet and hose

scant laundry accounts indicates that some monks at least chose to invest in them. In keeping with ideas of poverty and humbleness, the wool of the habit was supposed to be of a cheap and coarse kind, its colour perhaps deriving from the cheaper dark fleeces rather than dyed. In practice, however, there were some dyed broadcloths of fine quality on the backs of many monks.

LAYMEN'S CLOTHING

Laymen's clothes were also dominated by woollen fabric, but there the similarity ended. Most wore full-length leg hose, rather like a tight-fitting pair of trousers that also covered the feet. Instead of a zip fly, the gap at the front was covered by a 'cod piece' – a flap of cloth that pulled up over the opening and was tied at each side. The tighter the fit, the more prestigious and fashionable a person was trying to be. Labourers sported crudely cut, loose hose that required less skill to make, but were also less susceptible to wear and damage. Someone who saw their role more as a supervisory one could afford to sacrifice some practicality for a more individual fit, with cloth cut on the bias (a potentially wasteful use of material). Hose, however, were rarely made of the best cloth: they needed to flex and move with the wearer, so a looser weave was preferable and they wore out quickly.

Lacings were much more common as fasteners than buttons

The hose were held up by being tied to the doublet. This was a close-fitting garment, somewhere between a waistcoat and a jacket. Doublet and hose alone was still informal dress: for public life, a coat was also required. The coat, as the most visible garment, was generally made of the best cloth that could be afforded. It was a display item, as well as providing warmth, and was worn to church, to do business in and to entertain guests. Coat colours also respected this hierarchy of clothing. Dyed cloth cost more than undyed and white wool cloth, because it could be dyed, was more expensive than grey and brown sheep colours.

As a man of some substance but not unbounded wealth, Peter's hose were white undyed cloth, cut on the bias and close fitting. His doublet was made of linen canvas, again undyed, and was strong and cool to wear. They spoke to his position as a wealthy countryman, employing other labour whilst still having a practical, hands-on approach to running a prosperous

farming concern. Being Peter, he got rather more stuck in than some in his position might have and the hose certainly suffered as a result!

The close fit of both doublet and hose, perhaps counter-intuitively, gave Peter a freedom of movement which less fitted garments would have denied. The easy fit of modern clothing is only possible through the use of elastane and other stretchy manmade fibres. Where there is little or no give in the material, it is better to either have the garment follow the contours of the body closely so that it moves with the body or to have them very baggy indeed – as with monks' clothing – so that the body can move completely independently of the clothing.

Peter's coat was his only foray into the world of dyed cloth. Woad dyeing offered a range of shades, similar to those we are familiar with from jeans which are still dyed with the chemically identical indigo. Achieving a strong uniform blue is tricky: the washed-out blues are much simpler, take far less dyestuff and are much cheaper. The blue of Peter's coat was not a cheap one, but again suited his position as a successful member of the agricultural community. His outer clothing was completed with shoes, belt, purse and of course a hat, whilst underneath were linen shirt and breeches (I did the laundry so no garment was a mystery to me).

Tom, meanwhile, was eye-wateringly fashion forward, wearing his madder-dyed upper stocks rather than leg hose. In shape, they were just like a pair of leg hose that had been cut off at the knee and worn over another pair of rather simpler-shaped hose.

FOLLOWING FASHION

Keeping track of fashion at this date is not easy, particularly if you are interested in dress specific to one country or region. Most of the images we have for the time come from illustrated manuscripts produced almost exclusively in the low countries or France, or from woodcuts which are predominantly German. These bodies of work show very distinct differences in clothing between the three areas. As such, we can assume that English, Welsh, Irish and Scottish dress must have also been distinctive, but with very little evidence of what these regional differences actually were. Complicating matters further, the images and fragments of dress that do survive are heavily biased towards the wealthy and town dwellers.

My smock, grey kirtle and red gown

WOMEN'S CLOTHING

The cut of my own clothes crossed a divide. The gowns and kirtles (under dresses) of the 1480s and 1490s show long panels flowing from shoulder to hem, shaped to accommodate the curves of the human body. Those that appear in images of 1510 show a waist seam with a fitted bodice, joined to a separately cut skirt element. My kirtle was cut in the earlier style from some strong hardwearing grey-flecked kersey – the sort of wool produced from inferior, dark coloured, kemp filled fleeces. My gown was made out of a dyed, lightweight broadcloth, and was cut in a transitional style of about 1500 where the front panels remain in one from shoulder to hem, but the back has a seam across at waist height (the pattern came from a German tailor's book as there are none from England and I hope is a reasonable interpretation of what a comfortably-off peasant woman would have worn).

Under my kirtle and gown I wore a linen smock – a little like a shirt, but reaching down almost to my ankles. This formed the washable underwear, along with a short pair of hose that just came up to my knees and were tied with garters. My girdle (a woman's belt) was also an essential item of clothing. It not only supported my purse, but provided an anchorage for the skirts of my gown and kirtle – essential when I needed them up out of the way to get on with wet, muddy or dirty jobs.

HAIR
The injunctions in the Bible calling upon female modesty and covering the hair in the sight of the Lord were taken very seriously. The statement in St Paul's gospel that a woman's hair was her 'crowning glory and her husband's delight' was accurately reflected in early Tudor thinking. Women's hair was seen as a private, sensual pleasure, kept for her husband's eyes only.

Women's hair at this point in history was completely hidden from view. Once my hair was plaited and tied up out of the way, I wound a small band of linen around my head. I pinned it in place to control any wispy bits and to act as an anchorage for the veil. The veil itself was made of fine white wool, of a type still known as 'nun's veiling': it was lined with linen and pinned in place. Here, too, I could introduce a touch of fashion, and for no additional cost. In 1485, a woman would have smoothed the veil down so that it sat roundly about the forehead, but as images of the King's mother (the indefatigable Margaret Beaufort) show, English women had begun to wear their veils in a 'gable' style. You may be more familiar with it upon Catherine of Aragon some years later. For someone like me, the simple expedient of pinning the veil a little looser created the same shape, if not the same colours or materials, as that of wealthy court ladies.

Pins were another essential element of my dress. My headdress was entirely reliant on pins to hold everything together, with my gown also fastened at the front with them. This was common practice... and why a woman needed a little 'pin money'.

HOME CRAFTS

RUTH

The skills needed to equip a Tudor household are many and varied. Furniture, dishes and tools were all made by skilled craftsmen – and made to last. And even as simple a thing as light in the evenings would have been unheard of without the ability to craft rushlights from the by-product of life on the farm.

MAKING RUSHLIGHTS

Of all the options for providing light after dark, rushlights were the most economical. Candles could be made from beeswax or from tallow (the hard fat that collects around the organs of sheep), but both had their drawbacks. Beeswax was undoubtedly the best, but also the most expensive, and such candles were reserved for religious use. Tallow candles provided good light in wealthier domestic spaces, although they did smell when you burned them.

Rushlights utilised any spare fat left over from cooking, combined with free rushes picked from the ditches and river courses. You can use any species of rush that has a pith: mine came from some scruffy boggy ground near a stream. They were not the best I have ever used but at the tail end of the winter, when last year's growth is ragged and this year's flush has not yet got going, they were the best I could find.

The rushes are peeled, revealing the pithy core

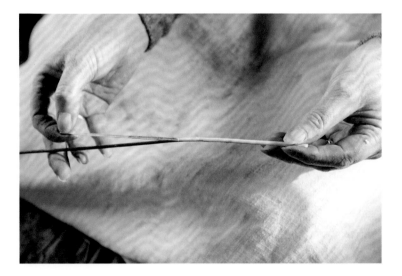

Each rush had then to be peeled, leaving a single continuous strip of the outer husk running the whole length of the rush, with all of the spongy white pith intact. The pith acts like a sponge, soaking up the fat but also providing it with a solid structure: the soft fat from the kitchen scraps would melt into

Rushlights give you about 20 minutes of illumination cheaply

a mess if it was unsupported (unlike the hard tallow or harder beeswax). The one remaining strip of rind acts as a wick, drawing melting fat to the base of the flame.

> ❝ IT WAS SOMETHING TO FILL IN SPARE MOMENTS, TO PROVIDE AN EXCUSE FOR A SIT DOWN AT THE END OF A BUSY TIRING DAY ❞

Preparing the rushes is a fiddly job, but not difficult; it was something to fill in spare moments, to provide an excuse for a sit down at the end of a busy tiring day. My fat came from the kitchen and was mostly mutton fat – not the top quality hard tallow, but the fat from a scrag end (the neck) of an old ewe who had reached the end of her useful, wool-producing life. I popped it into a pot with some water and left it to boil all day on the corner of the fire.

Gradually the fat melted into the water and rose to the surface. I left it to go cold overnight; the floating fat congealed into a solid layer that was easy to scoop off the surface, leaving the gristle and any scraps of meat or other tissues behind.

This clean (rendered) fat was popped into a dish and allowed to melt. Dipping the peeled rushes into the fat was quick and simple. Having laid them across another dish, they had soon solidified and were ready for use. The light that they give is as good as that of a candle, if a little smelly, but lasts only for 15 to 20 minutes and requires tending. Held vertically like a candle the rushlight goes out; held horizontally, it burns very quickly. An angle of around 60 degrees seems to give the longest burn time with the greatest reliability. You can hold it in your hand to light your way up to bed or you can put it into a holder to stand in the room. Even correctly positioned in its holder, it's best to glance over at it now and then to ensure that it's not dying down too much, that a curl of ash is not clogging the flame, or that its angle needs to be adjusted and a new one readied to replace it. Lighting a new rush in the dark with flint and steel is a right palaver, so it is better to light the new from the old before it burns away.

" YOU CAN HOLD IT IN YOUR HAND TO LIGHT YOUR WAY UP TO BED OR YOU CAN PUT IT INTO A HOLDER TO STAND IN THE ROOM "

If all this seems like a lot of work for such a little bit of light, then yes, it is. But if that is all you have got, then that is what you have to do.

Once peeled, the rushes are dipped in melted tallow

WOODEN BOWLS

The King might have eaten off silver and his lords off pewter dishes, but most people, whether monks or lay people, ate and drank out of wooden bowls. Such bowls were cheap, shatter proof, insulated and individual. They were made by professional wood turners working at a pole lathe and one could be found in every third or fourth village, supplying the local district. As well as wooden bowls to eat and drink out of, wood turners also produced platters and large bowls for use in the kitchen, brewhouse and dairy.

> ❝ WOOD TURNERS COULD BE FOUND IN EVERY THIRD OR FOURTH VILLAGE, SUPPLYING THE LOCAL DISTRICT ❞

We needed a good store of bowls, so I went off to see the appropriately named Robin Wood: the only professional pole lathe worker in Britain and a man with a passion for late medieval and early Tudor 'treen' (the correct word for wooden vessels of all shapes and sizes).

Robin Wood began by roughing out the blanks

Spinning the blank on the pole lathe, Robin began to shape the bowl

Robin began with freshly cut timber: logs around 30 to 40 cm in diameter cut to a similar length. Next, he cleft them into three for the larger logs and into two for the smaller ones. Most of us would expect a bowl to be made out of a slice through the trunk with the heartwood in the centre and the rim of the bowl following the outer ring of wood near the bark. However, as Robin pointed out, such a bowl or platter would split as the wood dried out.

By cleaving the log he could shape his bowl from the side of the tree with the base nearest to the heart and the rim closest to the bark, whilst the grain ran uniformly in one direction across the finished product. In use his bowls, like those that have been found in archaeological digs, would simply warp into a gentle oval shape, remaining strong and watertight throughout their long lives.

" ONE SLIGHTLY MISCALCULATED BLOW AND THE BOWL BLANK WOULD HAVE TO BE DISCARDED "

The cleft lumps were then shaped roughly with an axe. Watching Robin handle an axe with such precision and control was a joy: even as a well-practised producer of firewood, I know that I couldn't approach his level of skill. Robin at one point joked that 'it's the first thousand that are difficult'. One slightly miscalculated blow and the bowl blank would have to be discarded.

" IT'S THE FIRST THOUSAND BOWLS THAT ARE DIFFICULT "

Robin's lathe was a simple, solid affair. A long springy pole was fixed into the ground and bent over. Its free end was then tied with a piece of rope to a treadle and this rope was twisted once around the work. Held firmly between two metal spikes, our proto-bowl was able to spin freely.

The finished bowl felt wonderful – the sort of thing that you just have to run your hands around

When Robin pressed down upon the treadle with his foot, the string pulled down the pole, spinning the wood anticlockwise towards Robin. When he eased his foot off, the pole sprang back up spinning the wood in the opposite direction. Each press of the treadle made the wood spin three or four revolutions. Using hooklike tools (not gouges or chisels) Robin began to shape the spinning block. In doing so, he used his body weight, leaning in and out to change the direction as well as the intensity of the pressure on the tools as he worked.

The finished bowl was beautiful to hold. Sitting comfortably and warmly in my hands, it was a seemingly simple thing that hid a lifetime of skill in its making.

MEDICINE

Medicine of the early Tudor era was based upon a mixture of traditional remedies and ancient Greek thought. The medical manuscripts that circulated amongst scholars and physicians and were held in all the great libraries were texts that had been copied, compiled and recopied many times over. They derived from a mixture of Greek, Roman, Arabic and Hebrew texts in the main, although a few elements of Anglo-Saxon writings also crept in. Translated and retranslated, with exotic herbs replaced by local ones, the resulting recipes are something of a hotchpotch.

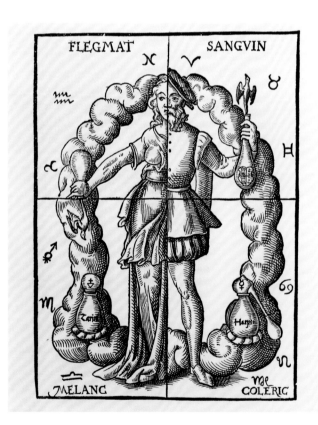

As the Renaissance began to make itself felt in these northern isles, scholars took a new look at the source manuscripts, with several writings that had been unknown in the West becoming newly available. These new studies would change the rationale of medicine, making ancient Greek ideas and theories clearer and more accessible to doctors. In 1475 when Henry VII came to the throne there was a rough idea, derived from the ancient authors, that all living things were ultimately formed of just four basic ingredients – or humours.

As time went on the details and a more rigid rationalisation of the system of thought developed, but this clarity is largely missing in the medical treatises of the last years of the 15th century and the first decade of the 16th. Much of the work undertaken by

A handy visual aid relating gender, astrology and alchemical principles to the four humours

THE FOUR HUMOURS

The four humours that humans were believed to be made up of were earth, water, fire and air: blood was hot and wet in its nature, the element of earth; phlegm was cold and wet in its nature, the element of water; yellow bile, hot and dry represented fire; black bile, which was cold and dry, formed the element of air. A florid-faced gentleman was thus seen as carrying more of the blood humour, a sallow-skinned person was biased towards the black bile, and so forth.

enterprising scholars of the next few years would be dedicated to fitting all the medical plants of these northern climes into the blood, phlegm, yellow and black bile classification. They looked at the plant, its key features and the medical uses it was put to in the traditional, partially ancient Greek texts. They theorised that each plant was dominated by one of the four humours, either mildly (in the first degree) or of a middling nature (the second degree) or was extremely strong in this humour or element (the third degree).

" THE TUDORS THOUGHT THAT ALL LIVING THINGS WERE ULTIMATELY FORMED OF JUST FOUR BASIC INGREDIENTS ~ OR HUMOURS "

Mustard, with its hot fiery taste, its usage as a cure for phlegm upon the chest and the sensation of heat that it gives when you eat a lot of it, seemed to indicate that this was a herb dominated by the yellow bile – the element of fire to the third degree. A plant like celery was a little more complex: its stems and leaves seemed cool, but its seeds could be warming; it also seemed to have a wetter nature rather than a dry one. Most scholars decided that it was a herb of the phlegmatic, cool and wet nature, close to the element of water, but only in the first degree. Its seeds, however, were said to be of the blood humour, a change that was brought about by the plant's affinity with the astrological sign of Leo. The role of astrology was an important one in medicine in the mid-Tudor period, with the ideas of Paracelsus and chemical medicine more influential at the very end of the Tudor period.

BLOODLETTING AND OTHER PRACTICES

For the most part, doctors and other medical practitioners at the start of the 16th century were content to follow the old collections of recipes without much in the way of unifying theories. They trusted that the 'ancient philosophers' offered tried and tested practices, the most important of which was bloodletting.

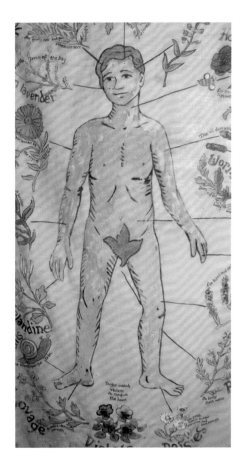

In order to understand the widespread use of leeches, cupping and cutting we must again look to the ancient idea of the four humours. If all people are formed of these four elements in perfect balance, then it follows that illness and disease are an expression of an imbalance. A person with a cold, for example, can be understood as someone for whom the phlegm humour has become overly dominant. Doctors would try to counteract the effects by adding the other elements to restore balance. Here, the cold wet nature of phlegm would be checked by taking medicine loaded with hot dry elements, such as mustard plaisters on the chest.

Another way to restore the balance would be to remove unwanted humours. In the case of a cold, frequent nose blowing would be sensible. Many physicians, however, would also be looking to promote urination to dry out the body: dandelion root, colloquially known as 'piss a bed', was often prescribed for its diuretic effects. With other illnesses, emetics were given to induce vomiting (yellow bile), laxatives to purge the black bile and bleeding to reduce blood levels. The hot, flushed, sweaty experience of fevers or high temperatures were all interpreted as an excess of blood; any sickness or disease that generated a high temperature as part of its pathology called for bloodletting.

Compiling extensive lists of plants and their medical properties, linking the astrology and humorial status, occupied some of the best scientific minds

MONASTIC HEALING

Monks and monasteries had a reputation for medicine and skill at healing. Certainly all monasteries had an infirmary for the care of their own elderly and sick. What actually went on in them is less clear. Herb gardens within monasteries rarely seem to have been very large in comparison to the size of the resident population, so we must be careful not to be drawn into the fictional world of Brother Cadfael in our imaginings.

❝ THERE IS, HOWEVER, LITTLE EVIDENCE OF MONASTIC MEDICAL SKILL: A MONK'S VOCATION WAS NOT THE CURE OF THE BODY BUT THE CURE OF THE SOUL ❞

There was certainly plenty of bloodletting, as this formed a regular part of the rule itself. Brothers were seasonally bled in order to lower their animal passions: the hot, wet blood humour was considered to be the direct cause of masculine virility and seasonal purification of the system was thought to aid a monk in living the religious life. There is, however, little evidence of monastic medical skill: a monk's vocation was not the cure of the body but the cure of the soul. Doctors were sometimes summoned to help sick monks and it was generally a hired-in lay professional who carried out the regular

Comfrey or 'knitbone'

bleedings. Though monasteries were very active in the distribution of charity, it was primarily food rather than medical care that they dispensed: the elderly and sick within the infirmary were permitted meat if they were thought to need it, even upon fasting days.

HOME HEALING

It would appear that monastic households had much the same attitude and response to medical provision as did other households: a basic range of herbs with a number of well-known medical recipes were fairly common knowledge and these were used domestically. Professional medical men, by contrast, could call upon a much larger array of plants and recipes, many backed with the authority of being derived from ancient authors. Apothecaries specialised in stocking this much larger pharmacopoeia, offering the plants in many different forms: plain-dried or turned into electuaries (honey based), salves (fat based) or distilled into waters and oils. Anyone could purchase their produce to augment their own herb garden supplies.

Over 2,000 plants were in regular medical use

For a price, doctors could offer diagnoses based upon examinations of people's urine, the nature of their symptoms and what they knew of their patient's general constitution. They consulted their books and recommended recipes or prescriptions that could be made up at home or by the apothecary. Such advice, however, was expensive and unavailable to most of the population. Domestic dosing, as a result, was the norm.

HOME REMEDIES

T he recipes available to both professional medical men and home remedy producers fell in to three basic categories: those that have some therapeutic use, the placebos and the downright dangerous. Even seemingly harmless recipes could cause health problems if the dosage is wrong, and with natural ingredients it is very difficult to tell how much of the active ingredients are present in any one plant or batch of medicine. The following recipes are interesting, but please don't try them at home!

FOR CORNS OF THE FEET (OR VERRUCAS)

'Take unslekkyd lyme and make small powder ther of and a quantitee of blake sope and medle hem togedir.'

A mixture of unslaked lime and cheap lye soap (no quantities are given) was to be laid upon the corn after you had sliced the top off it with a sharp knife. The mixture was to 'frete hym out'. Such a mixture would in fact work, burning away at the tissue, including the root of the verruca. However, I would not recommend that you try it as such a caustic concoction can cause serious chemical burns. Even the original recipe recommended caution, advising patients to use only a tiny amount and only upon the corn or verruca itself, carefully avoiding touching any of the surrounding skin. Once the burning was complete the area was to be covered in a mixture of egg yolk and honey to seal up the wound.

FOR THE MYGRAYNE

This recipe however falls into the second category, that of the placebo. A paste is made from pellitory and spikenard boiled in vinegar which is then mixed with honey and mustard. Half a spoonful of the paste is to be held in the mouth as long as the patient can bear and then spat out. This is to be repeated ten or twelve times after each meal. It is to be continued for four days and then you 'shalte be hole on warranties'.

I am a migraine sufferer myself, so the promise that I shall be whole, or cured in four days guaranteed, leaves me highly unimpressed. Even at their most violent none has ever lasted more than three days and for most people they are episodes that last for 24 hours. But I do understand that the hope of relief actually helps you cope minute by minute and that having something active to do about the pain also makes the experience more manageable.

FOR THE TOOTHACHE

'Take the sede of henbane and leke sede and encens by even porcion and lay hem on an hote glowynge tile stone.'

This cure for the toothache falls into the 'very dangerous' category rather than that of a placebo. The patient is required to suck the smoke into his mouth and while leek seed is not too noxious and neither is the incense, henbane is a very poisonous plant indeed. How much of the narcotic would be present in the smoke, I don't know. I guess that upon occasion the dosing was sufficient to provide pain relief but an overdose was an ever present possibility.

BEEKEEPING

PETER

In Tudor England, sugar was a luxury item. It was starting to be imported but was only found in very high society. Instead, honey was the main source of sweetness in food. As with so many important products, monasteries both produced honey, and also imported it from outside the abbey walls.

At the time bees were kept in 'skeps': these are conical baskets, usually made of straw (though sometimes with wattle and daub), placed open end down in which the bees make their combs. The word skep is thought to come from the Norse word skeppa, which is a container that could measure out a one half bushel. One thing bees don't like is bad weather so sometimes skeps are covered with cow dung or with a straw cone known

The monks checking the skeps

Oversized bees, hollow legs and a bear looking for honey

as a hackle. Sometimes buildings are built with special places to put skeps: these are known as bee boles. Bee boles have been recorded at various monastic sites in England. They are hard to date but it is thought they go back to around the 12th century. The building of bee boles shows that bees were being thought about at the time a particular structure was being built, though this does not mean that bees were not on the site before this. If anything, the bees were probably already being farmed and the bee boles were a convenient place to put some of the skeps. It is thought that the skep was developed in the Middle Ages and prior to this, a hollow log was used in order to farm bees.

There are depictions of clothing being worn that has a kind of wicker or straw face-guard for people inspecting bees. At the same time, with a fixed hive such as a skep, the amount of interaction that a bee-keeper would have with his bees is reduced. It is very hard to inspect the comb and the extraction of the wax and the honey endangers the colony. However, the time that bees are most likely to sting is when they are swarming around late May or early June. It is a brave person who is a bee-keeper with no protection and I think that even in the Tudor period bee suits of some description would have been worn.

BEES MAKE MONEY
Bee boles allowed bee-keepers to have a place to put a fresh swarm, enabling the bees to get used to almost constant human presence and allowed the owners to be able to keep an eye on their bees and if needs be lock them up at night. It was not only the honey that was valuable in the skep; the beeswax was a source of candles for the monastery as well as having a variety of other uses, and if a close eye was not kept on the bee hives often they would be rustled.

❝ THE TIME THAT BEES ARE MOST LIKELY TO STING IS WHEN THEY ARE SWARMING AROUND LATE MAY OR EARLY JUNE ❞

Tom's Diary

BEEKEEPING

The great thing about doing this farm project is getting to try out all sorts of new skills. Peter, Ruth and I would often count ourselves lucky when we thought about how, even in our bizarrest activities on the farm, many people would pay to get to do what we got to do. For me, beekeeping was one of those curious hobbies I would have paid to try. When asked whether I was allergic to bees, I smiled and said no. But on reflection, I realised I had never been stung by a bee, so I supposed that this was one way of finding out...

Honey is quite simply an amazing product. The colour is extraordinary when viewed in bright sunlight and close up. There is something visually mesmerising, too, about the way it moves. The only downside was the vast amount of bees that covered (admittedly their) honey, as Tudor clothing is not really designed for collecting such a substance. As nature's natural sweetener, honey's stickiness combined with wool clothing equalled a lot of mess. With mud you let it dry and it pretty much brushes straight off; with honey, you are more likely to encourage an ants' nest to pursue you across the fields. Wearing Tudor bee protection meant more layers and that meant heat became more of a concern than the bees.

No one wants to get stung but I'm a firm believer that as long as you do not upset most living things, then you have nothing to fear. Working out what might or might not upset a bee is complicated but I settled on making no sudden movements and only taking a percentage of the honey rather than clearing them out. Moving around the bees was not an issue but if anything unsettles you it is the noise the bees make. It seems inescapable when up close and does not seem to diminish as you move away, though merely a trick of the mind. The reward, though, for braving the bees is honey as organic as one could hope for with an incredible taste.

GARDENING FOR SUBSISTENCE

Standing at the end of the winter among the freshly dug beds of our garden, there was a palpable sense of excitement about the coming year. Everything was neatly laid out, raked and weeded, and I had a store of new marker sticks ready to deploy when I began to sow the season's seeds. It's no small feat to dig and rake that much ground, even when, as in this case, it is well maintained and already free from the perennial weeds and brambles that less cared for land is burdened with. We were lucky to have good soil that had been manured and worked for the last 40 years on a base of well-drained chalk, and it looked wonderful.

Our garden had to provide us with all the fruit and vegetables that we ate, with almost all the flavourings for our food, medicine, cleaning products, insecticides and home dyestuffs. Grocery shops in town sold dry goods rather than fresh food and even market stalls rarely included garden produce. The fact of this exerted its influence over everything that we did in the garden; we needed a rather different emphasis and ethos from that of the modern British gardener.

The gardener of 1500, whether provisioning a monastery or a family like ours, was looking for year-round yield: it was more important to have something to harvest in February than it was to have abundance in June. The total productivity of a garden had little relevance to most people. They grew species that were reliable rather than prolific and thought always of contingencies to deal with the possibility of crop failure.

Wild rocket and leeks were just two of the highly useful, and delicious, ingredients in our garden.

Well dug, raked and sown, our garden represented a huge amount of labour and of hope

CABBAGES

Cabbages were the most important vegetable of the period. A modern gardening manual will advocate cutting the whole head of the cabbage at its peak of perfection and varieties are selected for their propensity to form neat, large rosettes of leaves. This was rarely the Tudor way. Here, lower leaves would be individually plucked from the plant, allowing it to continue to grow upwards. This yielded a small but steady supply of the vegetable for use in the kitchen over a period of many weeks and even months. As the winter progressed, a cabbage patch became a forest of two-foot-high, thick knobbly stalks supporting the odd sprout of growth near the top. They didn't look particularly pretty, but they represented regular vitamin C throughout the leanest part of the year.

THE CASE FOR PERENNIALS

These survival priorities saw a preference for perennial plants over annuals, even though plants that grow fresh from seed each year are generally much more efficient at producing large quantities of edible matter. Annual plants have no need to husband resources to get them through the cold, dark months of the year and can instead concentrate their energies upon making the biggest show to attract insects and set the largest amount of seed. Modern gardening is almost entirely focused upon annual plants, from peas and beans to spinach and courgettes. Such seedlings, however, are very vulnerable to attack from the weather, pests and competition from other plants. As many of us have experienced, an entire crop can disappear overnight as the slugs move in or a late frost blackens off every shoot. If this was your only source of vegetable, it could be a disaster for the health and survival chances of your family.

> " AN ENTIRE CROP CAN DISAPPEAR OVERNIGHT AS THE SLUGS MOVE IN OR A LATE FROST BLACKENS OFF EVERY SHOOT "

For Tudor gardeners, it was therefore much more sensible to choose the lower yielding perennial plants that, once established, have tough, woody stems and cores and a much greater chance of surviving any onslaught. Carrots, with their susceptibility to carrot root fly and their temperamental germination rates, were a much rarer vegetable (and this is reflected in the surviving recipes) than skirrets. Skirrets are a root vegetable that have a similar flavour to carrots when they are raw, and to parsnips when they are cooked. They are small and white with a stringy core, but I think that they are delicious. The plant takes the form of a clump, and although you can grow them from seed (they need a period of sub-zero temperatures in order to germinate), they were generally propagated and harvested by dividing the clumps through the winter months, replanting smaller clumps and sending the rest to the kitchen. This method of growing provided reliability, even if you never achieved the bumper crops that a successful planting of carrots can give you.

A patch of woad in the corner of the plot

WEEDS

The other main difference between modern yield maximisation methods and earlier subsistence gardening was the treatment of weeds. A casual glance at our garden in high summer shows a riot of plant life, much of it consisting of 'weeds' and with a certain untidiness. This is deliberate. Some weeds are ruthlessly removed – those with no use – but others are allowed to remain as an edible backup to more conventional crops. Many common garden weeds, whilst not particularly tasty, are edible. Dandelions, nettles, fat hen and sow thistle were not crops as such, but should a few of your beans fail to come up, then rather than leaving an unprofitable space in the row, any weed that could be eaten that had established itself in the space was permitted to flourish. It was a careful balancing act between leaving weeds that could tide you through a hungry gap and removing those that threatened vigorous crops.

> "IT WAS A CAREFUL BALANCING ACT BETWEEN LEAVING WEEDS THAT COULD TIDE YOU THROUGH A HUNGRY GAP AND REMOVING THOSE THAT THREATENED VIGOROUS CROPS "

Fat hen among the Marlock beans

Weeding was a careful and thorough occupation, maximising the food output

Our blowsy, flowery, loosely growing garden represented an insurance policy, a hedging of bets against the vagaries of the weather and the attack of pests and diseases. Oh, and it looked beautiful! As the sun went down, slipping below the cloud layer and sending shafts of golden light along the length of the valley, the flowers would dance in the breeze. I could rarely resist a slow detour through the garden, nibbling on various leaves and blooms as I went, enjoying not just the visual delights but the incredible range of flavours that all these 'weeds' and crops have to offer. It is one of the sense memories that I know I will carry with me always.

GARDEN LAYOUT AND VARIETIES

PETER

A s part of our Tudor cottage and farmstead, we inherited a well-kept garden plot. This was divided into rectangular beds and fenced to keep out deer and other animals that might want to enjoy the fruits of our labours. The overall shape, layout and size of our garden reflected the images that appear in early maps and plans of villages and estates.

The gardens associated with palaces, castles and abbots' dwellings often show quite elaborately laid out beds: not quite the knot gardens of later years, but obviously designed for wandering through. Images of these same establishments generally show a second, larger plot in a much less prominent position, where the beds are bigger and laid out much more simply. The gardens of more modest folk follow this second pattern, representing not pleasure gardens, but spaces for the production of food and useful plants for the household.

Gardening advice in manuscript or print is a little scant. Fitzherbert's *Book of Husbandry*, for example, has only this to say:

> '*And in the begynnyng of March or a little afore, is tyme for a wife to make her garden, and to get a good many seedes and herbes as she can, specially suche as be good for the pot and to eate and as oft as neede shall requyer it must be weded, for els the wedes wyll overgrow the herbes.*'

However, there are also surviving lists of plants thought appropriate for the garden.

You can also look through recipes both for food and for medicine to get an idea of what people expected to have access to. Lists of medicinal plants could include two or three hundred species. Such extensive lists were rarely cultivated in one garden, but many people grew some of them and most could recognise many more, allowing them to gather them from the wild.

FOOD PLANTS

Alexanders, basil, beans, beet, borage, cabbage, caraway, carrots, chervil, chives, coleworts (which are another form of open hearted cabbage), cress, daisy and dandelion, fennel, Good King Henry, langedebeef, leeks, lettuce, marigold, marjoram, mint, nettles, onions, orach, parsley, parsnips, peas, purslane, radish, ramsoms (wild garlic), rocket, rosemary, sage, skirrets, sorrel, spinach, milk thistle, turnips and thyme.

CRAFTS, SKILLS & TRADE

Not only were the monasteries farming in the Tudor era, they were producing stonemasonry of the finest quality, experimenting with glass, venturing into iron and lead smelting, rearing fish on a huge scale and producing beer and wine. In fact, there were very few skilled professions in the 15th century that weren't associated in some way with the monasteries.

Although it was soon to be torn down in the dissolution, the monastic system went a long way to building society as we know it. Through their crafts and skills, our knowledge of materials came on in leaps and bounds.

THE CLOTH INDUSTRY

RUTH

t the start of the 16th century, cloth formed Britain's most important export and its most developed industry. It employed more people than any economic activity aside from agriculture and involved more movements of money than anything else – forming the basis of the proto-banking sector. Its organisation of labour and its technologies were complex.

Good English broadcloth was almost completely weatherproof

It hadn't always been that way. Way back before the Black Death, England in particular had been Europe's chief supplier of fine quality wool. Fleeces packed tightly into large sacks had made their way all across the continent to the best manufacturers. The wool that remained within our shores was generally the poorer grades and turned into basic serviceable cloth for the home market.

WOOL
Like most mammals, sheep produce two types of hair: a coarse, long fibre, which is shiny, stiff and sheds water; and a shorter, softer, finer under hair that provides insulation. It is the profusion of this second, softer sort of hair that makes sheep's wool so useful. The long shiny 'guard hairs' (called kemp when you are discussing fleeces) are hard to spin together and like to spring apart. The cloth they make as a result is coarse, harsh and itchy. English wool was prized for its lack of kemp, for its extreme fineness and for the crinkly nature of the woolly fibres – helping them to bind together and leave plenty of insulating air trapped between.

Cloth was Britain's most important export

The monasteries were an important part of this raw wool trade. They ran their flocks over vast areas, and were able to select both the best grazing land and rest pastures when necessary. The large size of their flocks made it a simple matter to select the best rams and keep the genetic stock high. The peasants' fleeces in contrast had to be gathered in a few dozen here, another dozen there by the merchant travelling around the countryside; their sheep had less choice of grazing and a restricted gene pool, all of which could significantly lower the wool quality.

> **" THE MONASTERIES WERE AN IMPORTANT PART OF THIS RAW WOOL TRADE "**

A large organisation such as a monastery could also afford to wait for its money whilst small farmers often needed the cash in order to pay the rent. It was another factor in favour of the monasteries: merchants offered higher rates for the 'dip' of the monks while negotiating deals to those in need of ready cash, paying a lesser rate for the fleeces whilst they were still upon the backs of the sheep. All in all monastic houses did well out of the raw wool trade.

THE RISE OF THE CLOTH INDUSTRY

By the end of the 15th century, the situation had changed: other nations were now also producing fine fleeces while at the same time Britain had begun to produce fine cloth to rival anything manufactured abroad. This shift had come about through the 'push' of difficult economic conditions and the 'pull' of the profits that came from selling premium goods. Rather than being an exporter of the raw material, Britain (not just England, but parts of Wales too) had become principally a manufacturer, exporting high value quality cloth across the known world. Most of the fleeces produced in Britain now fuelled the cloth industry, rather than making their way abroad.

Making cloth from wool was no quick process, and involved a lot of labour. Once sheared, the fleeces had to be sorted, combed and carded, spun and plied up into yarn. The yarn was then wound onto a warping frame and transferred onto a loom where the cloth could be woven. The 'web' was then washed, fulled and dyed. 'Fulling' was the process where the cloth was beaten with wooden hammers, to eliminate impurities and to thicken the fabric. By medieval times, it had been mechanised so that the fulling stocks, or hammers, were powered by a water mill. After fulling, the cloth was dyed, then stretched upon tenterhooks to prevent shrinking. The surface was then worked all over with teasel combs to raise a fluffy

Sorting the fleeces

Dyeing was a specialist task. Most professionals concentrated upon a small range of colours

nap, before shears were used to evenly cut off this nap to give a smooth even finish. All of these people needed to make a living from their labour and the full journey from fleece to sealed cloth upon the dockside was one of nearly a year. Cloth could not be a cheap commodity in such circumstances.

TYPES OF CLOTH

The premium product was 'broadcloth' – it was 'broad' because it was woven double width. A standard loom – such as the one I helped set up – was worked by one person who needed to be able to reach from one side to the other comfortably in order to throw the shuttle back and forth: this gave a cloth of around 28 inches wide (perhaps 71 cm). Broadcloth, by contrast, was woven on a loom that could make cloth 60 inches wide (152 cm) and needed a second person, usually a child, to throw the shuttle back from the far end. Such cloth was woven from high quality yarn that offered the very finest crimped fibres: this could only be obtained from certain types of sheep, reared and grazed on certain types of pasture. Once woven, the cloth was fulled, and the nap raised and sheared. This changed the cloth from a visible weave through which light could be seen to a dense, sheer fabric, which was felt-like in appearance. The finished cloth was virtually weatherproof, shedding rainwater, and also windproof. Unlike true felt, it was flexible and hard-wearing.

> ❝ THE FINISHED CLOTH WAS VIRTUALLY WEATHERPROOF, SHEDDING RAINWATER, AND ALSO WINDPROOF ❞

'Scarlet' was an even more expensive product than broad-cloth – the word denoting a cloth type before it came to mean the colour. This was fulled and sheared like broadcloth but was much lighter and finer: good scarlet (and it was often dyed a vivid red) was soft and fine enough to draw through a man's thumb ring. Also made was 'kersey' – cheaper and narrow-width, it was intended largely for the home market rather than export, but some still found an international market.

INTERNATIONAL TRADE

The centre of international trade for British cloth was London. Merchants from across the land would send their finished lengths of cloth to be checked, sealed and sold. Maintaining quality was essential to protect market confidence in the product, to keep its price high and the repeat business rolling in. To this end, rules and inspections were strict: cloth for international sale had to be exactly the correct width and pieces exactly the right length. The overall piece also had to weigh a certain amount without the addition of 'dressing', be free of holes or other faults and the dyes 'true' shades and even. Only when the officials were happy that all the criteria had been met would they affix the lead seal to the end of the cloth, denoting it fit to be traded.

SPINNING, WEAVING & DYEING WOOL

RUTH

Turning individual fibres into yarn is a truly ancient art, perhaps older than the taming of fire and the fashioning of blades. Just twisting them in your fingers turns a bundle of short, crudely aligned, individually weak strands into a long strong thread. Adding fibres into the untwisted end of the bundle allows you to make a longer and longer yarn. The use of drop spindles had been speeding up the process for several thousand years but by 1500 another technological development was also well under way.

Cutting-edge textile technology

THE SPINNING WHEEL

I am not the world's best spinner. My yarn breaks at times and uneven lumps have been known. I do, however, spin enough to know what a significant breakthrough the spinning wheel was, as well as its limitations. Even in my semi-skilled hands, the wheel triples the speed of thread production.

A drop spindle is simply a weight on a stick. You give it a twist (like a spinning top) with your working hand whilst holding the untwisted end of your fibre bundle in the other hand. Once it is set spinning, you can use both hands to draw out a few fibres, then let go at the spindle end to allow the twist to travel up the new section, binding them into new yarn.

As you work, your yarn gets longer until the spindle reaches the ground. At this point you

*Most yarn was produced
by women, especially those
unmarried with less domestic
tasks. This led to them being
linked to this task - the 'spinster'.*

have to stop and wind the newly made thread onto the spindle, then start
again with the spindle suspended just a few inches from your fingers. The
drop spindle is straightforward, cheap and very controllable. It is also
very slow.

Enter the spinning wheel. The spindle has now been turned through 90
degrees and held in place by a wooden frame. Instead of powering the twist
with a flick of your fingers a much longer lasting spin is achieved with a fly
wheel. This wheel is held in place, close to the spindle, by the frame, with a
piece of cord running around the wheel spindle in
a loop, forming a drive band. Flick the wheel with
your hand and it spins the spindle.

> **" A REALLY GOOD SPINNER (OR
> SPINSTER IF YOU ARE FEMALE)
> CAN WALK BACK AROUND
> 20 FEET ON EACH RUN "**

Working with a long spin and a horizontally set
spindle, it is possible to produce very long lengths
before you have to stop and wind it on. Beginning
next to the spindle, you set the wheel in motion
and walk backwards at an angle from the wheel, drawing out the fibres
and letting the twist bind them. Just as the wheel is running out of power
you bring your arm, and yarn, round to a plane parallel with the wheel: the
thread is automatically wound onto the spindle guiding your footsteps back
to where you began.

A really good spinner (or spinster if you are female) can walk back around 20 feet on each run. Going backwards and forwards all day long, it is no wonder that this style of wheel is often called a walking wheel.

If you twist a length of fibres in your fingers, you will see how the twisting strengthens and binds, but you will also notice that as soon as you let go it all comes undone. However, if you fold your twisted length in half and then let go it twists back on itself and stays in place. This is called plying the yarn.

Take two lengths of yarn, both twisted in the same direction, lay them next to each other and twist them the opposite way together – you now have a stable, two-ply yarn that won't unravel and can be woven up into cloth.

> **" THE SPINNING PROCESS IS SO TIME CONSUMING ~ AROUND TWELVE TIMES AS LONG AS THE WEAVING "**

Even a few blades of grass can demonstrate basic yarn technology

Two strands twisted, then allowed to twist back on themselves creates a stable yarn

The spinning process is so time consuming – around twelve times as long as the weaving – that anything that eased the bottleneck opened up large opportunities for growth. Spinning wheels significantly cut the price of cloth production and increased the national output. But despite being a great step forward, they could not do everything.

The yarn that the spinning wheels produced so quickly was soft and loosely spun, perfect for the weft of a fabric (the threads that pass back and forth across the web) but not strong enough for the warp (the threads that run along the length of the web and are fixed on the loom). Plying up the yarn was easier to achieve with the old drop spindle. As a result, the best cloth in 1500 was made of a mixture of drop spindle spun warp and wheel spun weft: the warp providing strength and the weft making it warm, soft and fluffy enough to be fulled and sheared into a perfect, smooth finish.

LOOMS

Looms had also been evolving. The 'counterbalance treadle loom' had come to dominate production right across Europe, and this was the type of loom that I helped to set up to weave our yarn.

The warp threads were wound onto a beam held at the back of a large wooden frame about the size of a four-poster bed, then brought horizontally forward to be wound onto a second beam at the front. On their journey from the back to the front of the loom, each individual thread passed through two shafts which could lift alternate threads; they then passed, in pairs, through the 'reed' which held them evenly apart across the width of the fabric. The two shafts were connected to the treadles so that the weaver could raise first one set of threads and then the other set of threads by pushing down on the appropriate treadle. The reed was free to move horizontally, rather than vertically and was used to beat each new pass of the weft thread back into place.

❝ IT'S A VERY SIMPLE SET OF MOVEMENTS REPEATED OVER AND OVER ❞

Once the meticulous business of threading all of the warp threads had been done, and the tension of each thread adjusted, the weaver sat and took a shuttle loaded with yarn. As one foot depressed a treadle, half the threads rose and the other half were left in place; the shuttle passed through the gap (called the shed) between the alternate threads leaving a single line of yarn behind. The foot was then lifted from the treadle and the reed was brought forward, easing the yarn into place. Now the second treadle was employed to raise the other set of warp threads, with the shuttle passing between that gap and the reed again, pushing the weft thread into place.

It's a very simple set of movements repeated over and over. The skill lies in keeping the tension perfectly even throughout the full length of the cloth – work that continues for weeks. Such perfect precision of movement takes a great deal of practice, a fact which explains why weavers were professionals. Anyone can weave a rough piece of wonky cloth, but something good enough for sale was a different beast entirely, and after all that work spinning, few people were willing to spoil their yarn with home weaving. Even for workaday cloth for use in the home, it was well worth taking your yarn to the professional.

> ❝ ANYONE CAN WEAVE A ROUGH PIECE OF WONKY CLOTH, BUT SOMETHING GOOD ENOUGH FOR SALE WAS A DIFFERENT BEAST ENTIRELY ❞

The fulling stocks in action, tightening and felting the cloth

The loom that wove our cloth was the most common type in use. It was a very simple one and could turn out the basic weave (tabby) quickly and fairly cheaply. Elaborate weaves, by contrast, required a machine of far greater complexity.

The addition of more shafts allowed twills and herringbones to be produced; a draw loom with a comber board and pulley box could produce pictures in cloth. Its use of binary code to control the output, determining the pattern, prefigured the first computers. The stunning silks and velvets produced upon such machines take your breath away. The best modern computer-controlled looms struggle to replicate these fabrics; if there were not surviving examples of the cloth, it would be hard to believe that they were achievable in 1500.

FULLING TECHNIQUES

Such technological wonders were continental, particularly Italian. The British industry focused not upon amazing weaves but upon the finishing of woollen cloth. The vast majority of home woven fabric was fulled: this is a washing, shrinking process that knits the fibres closely together,

Deafening and dangerous though it was, the cloth was fulled in a fraction of the time that it would have take by hand – or foot

making the weave pattern almost completely invisible.

You can full cloth by hand or, more commonly, by foot. The cloth is put into water along with a generous handful of fuller's earth – particularly absorbent clay – and bashed around vigorously. The cloth becomes fluffy and shaggy as fibre ends work their way loose. The dirt and natural sheep grease comes out of the wool and as the whole cloth shrinks, the fibres are tightly entwined together. The more vigorous the action the more fibre ends are available to bind like this, creating a stronger and denser mesh.

" THE VAST MAJORITY OF HOME WOVEN FABRIC WAS FULLED "

By 1500, almost everyone fulled their cloth by machine (except for some of the far-flung corners such as the Isle of Harris, where they were still using their feet and hands in the early 19th century). The machines were water powered and consisted of wooden hammers beating the cloth laid in wooden troughs. The noise, as I discovered when I took ours to the mill, was deafening and the whole building shook. With a little scaling up such stamping mills would later be used for crushing ore and powering huge hammers in industrial forges. As with so many technologies and industrial practices, their life began in the textile industry.

The water wheel turned a thick horizontal shaft, embedded with a series of large wooden pegs, set in a staggered pattern. The large wooden hammers (metal would have damaged the cloth as well as costing a good deal more) were drawn up by the pegs as the shaft rotated, and allowed to drop as the shaft turned further.

WOOD TYPES

The type of wood used for each part of the machine had a big impact upon its resilience and efficiency. Pines would have leaked sticky sap onto the cloth and soft woods in general would have quickly rotted in the permanently wet environment. Chestnut is particularly rot resistant and ash generally copes better with the shaking than oak. Elm, too, was much liked for shafts, but pegs wore away too quickly unless they were made of the very toughest of timber. Willow was just as good for hammers as it would become for cricket bats: resilient to hard shocks, but smooth grained and mostly splinter free.

Wet and misshapen from the fulling trough, cloth had to stretched out to the regulation size and have its evenness restored by attaching it to large drying frames (or tenters) with tenterhooks. The fulled cloth then had its nap raised with teasel combs and was sheared smooth – in the case of scarlets, this process was repeated four times to achieve the very best of finishes.

" THE BLACKSMITH WHO COULD MANUFACTURE SUCH SHEARS WAS TRULY A MASTER OF HIS TRADE "

The shearing was an especially skilled process: three-foot-long blades were manipulated to evenly cut a millimetre or less of fluff off a full length of expensive woven cloth, without ever nicking or cutting it. The blades had to be absolutely level and perfectly set so that exactly the same degree of pressure was required to cut along their entire length. The blacksmith who could manufacture such shears was truly a master of his trade.

The blue of Peter's coat came from the fermented leaves and stems of the woad plan

DYING WOOL

Most of the cloth produced for export was 'dyed in the piece', meaning that it was dyed after it had been woven and fulled. In some areas of the country, around us in West Sussex for example, it was more usual to 'dye in the wool' – dyeing the fleeces before they were combed, carded and spun. This gave the opportunity for the comber and carder to blend colours before they were spun. It produced an especially dense rich colour in the finished cloth as the dye penetrated right to the heart of the fabric; those that were dyed in the piece often retained an undyed core to the cloth, with the dye lying only upon the surface.

Naturally, dyeing in the wool was more expensive, using up far more dyestuffs, so it was reserved only for the finest wool being made into the most costly cloth. Cloth that was dyed 'in the yarn' was less common and generally confined to coarser, cheaper goods. The spun yarn was dyed before being woven up and this allowed weavers to produce striped and checked cloth. Welsh wools for local use were often dyed and striped in this fashion and Scotland too already had a tradition of checked, or plaid, fabrics.

BUILDING CRAFTS

Our cottage might have looked rustic (our own building efforts certainly were), but beneath the humble exterior of our Tudor buildings, there was a lot of Tudor technology at work. What's more, the signature of medieval architecture is still plain to see in castles and cathedrals across Britain. Day to day buildings such as houses tended to be crafted from timber, wattle and daub, while high status structures were made from stone – but all required a great deal of craft and skill in the making.

A mason's carving of a lion passant supporting a stone keep

STONEMASONRY

After the departure of the Romans, stone wasn't used as a major building material in Britain until the arrival of the Normans. Even then, the buildings that were constructed from stone were usually high status.

Each of these stone buildings would have had a resident mason and when looking at Tudor stonemasonry I met the master mason Pascal Mychalysin at Gloucester Cathedral. Pascal was trained in France with skills that have been passed down from generation to generation and when he came to England and met masons over here, he found that they too had the same way of holding and using tools. Because sheet metal was relatively rare in Tudor England, masons didn't cut stones using saws but used axes instead. In order to guide the axe, get a precise cut and put a face on a stone, Pascal showed me that you place your index finger on the blade. There is a stone carving in Norwich Cathedral of a stonemason using an axe in precisely this way.

In my mind I have always considered stone as a relatively hard material, but like wood it has to season. When stone is first cut from the quarry, there is

Gloucester Cathedral. The beauty and softness of stone is accentuated by the skill of the mason

a window of around two months while there is still sap or moisture in the stone. If the mason cuts the stone in this time then it is like cutting through butter. Stone could therefore be cut out of the quarry, transported to the building site, dressed in situ and then hauled up and put in place to harden. One exception to this is in France, where a chalky limestone when cut is left on the flood plain of a river to be washed for ten years before use.

When building structures like cathedrals, which are ornately decorated, masons tended to favour free stones – stones that can be cut in any direction. Many of the designs that they carve out of these stones require a strong understanding of geometry, spacial awareness and the ability to think in three dimensions. Over the years, masons have been associated with secret societies: the idea that their skills can only be passed down to certain people. In reality, the tools and techniques are little changed and open for all to see. However, life was hard and often short for stonemasons and the buildings they were constructing could take decades to build. This gave them little time to pass on their skills so they only bothered with the apprentice masons that they knew had the abilities. Basically, anyone could be a stonemason in the same way that anyone can be a top-flight footballer: the only requirement is that you have the talent.

WOODWORKING

Everyday buildings like houses, including our own, were generally built out of wood. When wood is buried in the ground, it will eventually rot but around the start of the 13th century it appears padstones were starting to be used. Padstones are stones upon which principal timbers can rest: this stops them having to be buried so the likelihood that they will rot is dramatically decreased. The result is that there are several surviving timber-framed buildings from the Tudor period.

Timber-framed buildings can generally be divided into four types: box-framed, post and truss, aisled and cruck-framed. Box-framed is a fairly loose category but it is generally accepted that these are buildings where no purlins are used in the roof construction, with the rafters just sitting on top of the wooden box instead. Post and truss is similar to box-framed, except that it uses purlins and truss posts in the roof construction: if a single post is used, this is a king post but if a wider area has to be spanned two posts, known as queen posts, are used. Aisled construction, meanwhile, is simply an expansion on the box-framed type, with either side being flanked by two side aisles. Cruck-framed, by contrast, is a very distinctive building style.

Bayleaf farmhouse with its now 'classic' Tudor wooden-frame structure

Note the pegs in this roof, which will be pushed through off set holes to tighten the joints

In its true form it consists of a single curved timber that has been split in half and spans from the apex of the roof to the ground. This means that the weight of the roof is supported by these timbers and the walls are not necessarily load bearing. A full cruck doesn't need tie beams.

When constructing timber-framed buildings Tudor carpenters would seek out the smallest trees that they needed to complete the job. This reduced the amount of wastage and also the amount of effort it took to make the timbers.

> **THE TIMBER WOULD TWIST AS IT DRIED, LOCKING ALL THE JOINTS TOGETHER**

The wood was generally 'worked green' (freshly cut) by sawing (either over a pit or on trestles), hewing (squaring off a side of timber by using an adze axe) and riving (splitting the wood along the grain). When the building was built using green wood, it would season over a period of time. The timber would twist as it dried locking all the joints together and giving Tudor buildings their characteristic higgledy-piggledy look.

DAISY WHEELS

Some Tudor buildings may look like they were put up in the dark, especially compared with modern millimetre-perfect construction techniques. However, there is definitely a science behind the art. Often in buildings of both wood and stone geometrical patterns known as daisy wheels are found etched in the fabric. These patterns are made using a compass and usually comprise circles and petals. There is an argument that they were etched on buildings in order to ward off evil spirits and this may be so, but equally there is a very strong argument that they were used in order to determine the angles and the shapes of the building being constructed.

Geometric daisy wheel, sometimes known as a mass wheel

Looking at the patterns, they are clearly very pretty. When you go on to see the squares, triangles, hexagons, the 180-degree compass divided into 15-degree increments and so on, it is a very compelling case that they were involved in construction. I have read that some of these daisy wheels are found in places that are virtually inaccessible but what I know from building myself is that, firstly, you often find yourself crammed into spaces that only trained circus folk should try to enter and secondly, calculations are often done on materials that have yet to be put in situ. On numerous occasions, I have been writing on a piece of timber or plaster board and using it as a guide up until the point that it is time to use it; at which point, another piece of lumber becomes my calculation pad.

> « OFTEN IN BUILDINGS OF BOTH WOOD AND STONE GEOMETRICAL PATTERNS KNOWN AS DAISY WHEELS ARE FOUND ETCHED INTO THE FABRIC »

I don't know if either the superstition or calculation theories are true. They may both be off the mark but, equally, there is a possibility that they both hold credence. Perhaps not only does the daisy wheel aid in the calculations required in construction but also wards off evil after the building is built. If it was the latter, Tudor builders wouldn't be alone in their superstitions: to this day builders in Germany place a pine tree on top of a building until it has a roof on, in order to keep away bad spirits.

GLASS MANUFACTURE

If you were to survey 100 people and ask them what a window was I wonder how many of them would mention glass? I know I would, but technically a window is a portal and in a building its purpose is to let in the light. Glass is just the fantastic material that allows that to happen while also keeping out the weather.

In modern society we are surrounded by glass as it is one of our primary construction fabrics (just consider the ever changing London skyline). In early Tudor England, however, it would have been a high status material.

Not all windows have glass in them

Prehistoric man made tools from obsidian which is a naturally occurring volcanic glass, and flints that are found in chalk are not too dissimilar in their behaviour. The first glass is thought to have been made in the ancient Near East and the Romans certainly had a large number of glass artefacts, including windows. However, it was in Sussex that broad sheet glass was first produced in 1226. This was done by blowing molten glass, using a blowpipe, into a large balloon shape and then, while the glass is still hot, cutting it open and flattening it out.

Beautiful art framed by hard-won lead

This resulted in a poor quality glass that was often opaque with pock marks and scars where it had been flattened out. However, it was glass and it could then be combined with lead cames to make leadlights. A century later, French glassmakers in Rouen were perfecting what was to be known as crown glass: this is the glass that looks like the base of a bottle. The next major leap in glass manufacturing was the production of blown plate glass in the 1620s in London, a process which involved grinding and polishing broad sheet.

Monasteries became major consumers of glass in the later Middle Ages but it doesn't appear that they were heavily involved in the craft. The glassmakers of the Weald were largely left alone by the monasteries, who both used their glass and also imported it from France. The idea of using glass in a church was both a means of letting in the light of God but also controlling the light and what could be seen.

Soon the glass was giving way to stained glass to make up illuminated wall decorations. Many monasteries employed craftspeople to paint the clear glass, which must have looked stunning.

> **" USING GLASS IN A CHURCH WAS BOTH A MEANS OF LETTING IN THE LIGHT OF GOD BUT ALSO CONTROLLING THE LIGHT, AND WHAT COULD BE SEEN "**

Today, stained glass is a term that we use to refer to all coloured glass but technically it is glass that has had its chemical composition altered during the manufacturing process. Thousands of these windows were destroyed after the dissolution of the monasteries, firstly by Henry VIII who wanted the lead and then by the puritan Oliver Cromwell who saw them as an insult to God.

TUDOR TRADESMEN

BLACKSMITH

Blacksmithing really started to take off in the Tudor period. They could make any tools that they needed from a starting point of an anvil, a hammer and a pair of tongs.

GLAZIER

More and more windows were being glazed and this was a new skill, blowing and cutting glass.

CARPENTER

Wood was the predominant building material and with the population expanding, houses would have to be built. The skill in carpentry was getting the most out of the wood on its journey from forest to timber-frame building.

PLASTERER

Whether plastering directly onto lathe or skimming onto wattle and daub, it is the plaster that finishes off that classic Tudor building look. However, it is the mock Tudor styles popularised during the Victorian period that have our minds thinking in black and white. Plasterers when slaking their lime would add tallow for waterproofing and often a pigment for colour.

THATCHER

A good thatched roof can last between 10 and 30 years, depending on the location and materials. Wooden buildings and thatched roofs had been outlawed in London prior to the Great Fire of 1666 but the fact that they were being used demonstrates their popularity.

SLATER AND TILER

Although thatch is a great roofing material it is best suited to areas of large arable land. In areas of slate, such as parts of Wales, it makes more sense to use this instead.

BRICKLAYER

Brick was a high status building material in Tudor England and was used to build, among others, Cowdray Park near our farm and Hampton Court Palace. Tudor bricklayers were known for their ornate patterns. Later in the Tudor period, in 1571, the first standard of brick size was set.

STONEMASON

Not only did stonemasons build and repair stone buildings, they also decorated them. Their ornate carvings often softened and added interest to the appearance of what is otherwise a very hard material.

WINDMILLS

PETER

Wind power has been in use by mankind for millennia but the origins of the windmill remain unclear. It is thought that early examples date back to 9th-century Persia, but in England windmills were only in use from around the 12th century.

The restored post mill in Worthing

The earliest windmills in England were post mills, with sails vertical to the ground that drive the mill stones. It is known as a post mill as the whole mill pivots on a central post. It does not have a fantail, so in order for the sails to face the wind the miller has to physically move the whole structure.

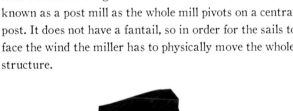

THE DAILY GRIND
'The daily grind' is a term that originally refers to the process of grinding flour to make bread on a daily basis. This would have taken place on a quern stone, which is essentially a rough stone upon which grains can be placed. By using a hand-stone, they can be ground into flour. It is thought that this is also where the term 'nose to the grindstone' comes from.

The inside of a windmill – the height of Tudor technology

For this reason the size of post mills is limited but even then some are still larger than others. The one we used to grind our grain was the High Salvington Windmill on the outskirts of the Sussex coastal town of Worthing. The sails of this windmill are a whopping 58 feet in diameter. There has been a mill on the site of High Salvington since at least 1615 but by the end of the Victorian period it had been closed as a commercial mill. It was destined to rot in the mill field, had it not been for a group of mill enthusiasts who looked over the gate in 1976. They persuaded the council to let them restore the mill to working order and over the next 15 years or so set about the task of doing so.

SETTING SAIL

Peter Casebow has been involved with the mill restoration since day one and he showed me just how a Tudor post mill would have been used. The first job the miller has is to set the sails. The earlier form of sails was the common sails, which are wooden trestle frames which are covered with a sail cloth. The sails can be trimmed much the same as sails of a ship are trimmed, so that there is less fabric covering the trestle in higher winds. The only problem with this was that the miller had to stop the sails and climb up in order to adjust them.

Once the sails are set, the whole structure of the windmill has to be turned to face the wind. This is done using a lever by the stairs. The stairs lift off the ground, the mill is pushed and then the stairs are lowered back to act as an anchor keeping the mill facing in the desired direction. If the wind is blowing sufficiently fast the brake can be removed and the post mill comes to life. I have been inside plenty of water mills but I had never been inside a windmill before (especially one that is balancing on a single post in the ground). It is much the same as being on a wooden sailing ship. The whole structure is moving and the wood is creaking and groaning as it flexes.

" BEING INSIDE A MILL IS MUCH THE SAME AS BEING ON A WOODEN SAILING SHIP. THE WHOLE STRUCTURE IS CREAKING AND GROANING AS IT FLEXES "

MILLING

To start milling, grain is brought up to the top of the mill with a winch that runs off the power of the sails. The bags are brought up from ground level through trap doors in the floor to the hoppers situated just above the millstones.

When the grain begins to run low, a bell attached to the hopper falls and rings, alerting the miller. If the miller does not either add more grain or disengage the stones and the grain runs out, the millstones rub together. This not only wears away his millstones but also produces sparks. Flour dust in the air is highly explosive and if one of these sparks ignites, then the miller may find himself working in the big mill in the sky.

Gritstones can grind around 100 tonnes of flour before they need to be re-dressed by a stonemason. Other stones used are made of French burrstone, which is a hard, coarse-grained limestone. These stones were often assembled in pieces and held together with metal bands and they can grind around 500 tonnes of flour before needing attention.

A thatched granary on staddle stones to deter rodents. Another Tudor method of rodent repellent was placing sheaves on a bed of prickly goose

Amidst the hunt, a water miller brings in his grain

The power of the windmill is immense and once the wind picks up the flour pours out. The mill would have had a slide at the back of the stairs so that once the bags were full they could be slid back to the ground and taken to the granary to be stored prior to transport.

TAKING THE HIGH GROUND

A major feature of windmills is that they needed to occupy the high ground to make full use of the wind. This meant that they could be seen for miles around and therefore they were used as a means of passing messages. At the end of each day, the sails were left in the form of the cross of St Andrew, which was the best way to shed water and puts the least amount of stress on the sails; at the start of the next day, the sails would be placed in the form of the cross of Christ. Births could be announced as well as deaths, and the news that the Spanish Armada was coming in 1588 was said to be signalled by Heene Mill.

" FLOUR DUST IN THE AIR IS HIGHLY EXPLOSIVE "

As towns grew and industrial mills were built, many of the windmills were either moved or were dismantled or left to rot. Dotting the landscape and often kept alive by enthusiasts, mills such as the black post mill at High Salvington still survive. Recently, too, there has been an upsurge in the demand for flour milled by stone rather than rolled through metal. They remain an ongoing part of our heritage.

BLACKSMITHING &
THE BLAST FURNACE

PETER

ron (and what we now call steel) has been one of the most important materials on earth for the advancement of mankind and society. It is one of the most abundant elements in the earth's crust, but very rarely occurs in its pure form. Instead iron is usually bound over with other materials in what we call iron ore. Extracting it is a science mankind has been perfecting for thousands of years.

ANY OLD IRON

The Iron Age (1200 BC–AD 400) gets its name because this is when it is accepted that our ancestors were beginning to understand how to separate and work the metal. In order to remove iron from iron ore, it needs to be heated and this was originally done in a furnace known as a bloomery. Most bloomeries look very similar to an anthill and are generally conical in shape like a chimney. At the base there will be one or two pipes known as tuyères, penetrating into the centre of the bloomery so that air can be pumped in. Charcoal is used as it is a fuel that is almost pure carbon and has very few impurities and this heats the iron ore. Once the bloomery is in operation, additional fuel and ore can be fed into the furnace from the top.

Out of the bottom of the furnace comes both slag (which is all the waste products) and a spongy mass known as a bloom. Iron has a very high melting point – 1,538°C – but it is also an allotrope. This means that unlike water which is solid at one temperature and liquid at another, iron can inhabit both states. Between the temperatures of 912°C and 1,400°C the material is going through a phase transition from solid to liquid. The bloom that comes out of the furnace is essentially iron in this state. Through reheating it and hitting it with hammers – a process known as wroughting – molten slag can be driven out and carbon, which hardens the metal, can be introduced.

BLAST FURNACES

The next step in iron production was to 'pimp the bloomeries'. Temperatures had to be reached and sustained so that iron ore could not just be heated but so the iron itself could be melted into a liquid. This required a massive influx of oxygen using a piece of apparatus known as a blast furnace.

Blast furnaces were bigger and taller than bloomeries (essentially around eight-foot-square chimneys) and the air was forced in by the use of water-powered bellows. This led to greater temperatures and iron being produced on an industrial scale. However, unlike self-fluxing bloomeries (a flux gets rid of impurities during smelting), limestone had to be added in order to form a slag. At the end of the process the molten iron was tapped off and would run out into channels, resembling a sow with suckling piglets (this gave rise to the term pig iron). Pig iron is an intermittent stage of iron production and is very brittle. When worked in a finery forge (which would usually be on the same site), it could be made into bar iron for use by blacksmiths. Perhaps more importantly pig iron can also be turned into cast iron for applications such as pots, pans, cannons, firebacks and any other metal object that has to potentially deal with high temperatures.

THE ORIGINS OF THE BLAST FURNACE

It is thought that the Chinese had the ability to liquefy iron as early as the Zhou Dynasty (1122–256 BC). In Europe, however, the technology is thought to have taken off only in the late Middle Ages (1350–1500). A common misconception is that the blast furnace was introduced to the UK by Abraham Darby in 1709 in Coalbrookdale. In fact, he perfected the use of coke as a fuel to replace dwindling charcoal supplies, boosting an industry that left cast iron structures in its wake. It is generally accepted that the first British blast furnace was built around 1490 near Buxted, during the reign of Henry VII.

Be it Tudor, be it Victorian, be it modern – the fire that forges is timeless

These advancements in the use of iron and its applications are similar to how our descendants will look upon 3D printing. Farmers and monks were very involved at the cutting edge of iron technology and the subsequent experiments and investment in iron production facilities helped make some monastery land very attractive to purchasers following the dissolution.

Certainly, the Cistercian monks were skilled metallurgists and are thought to have aided the spread of blast furnace technology. Investigations are still ongoing as to the extent of their technology, especially in places like Laskill in North Yorkshire near the ruins of Rievaulx Abbey. However, the best working example of the Tudor technology that we could find was the furnace at the Rural Life Centre Museum in Tilford.

> ❝ IRON PRODUCTION NOT ONLY CHANGED THE FACE OF BRITISH MATERIAL CULTURE, IT ALSO CHANGED THE LANDSCAPE ❞

Iron production not only changed the face of British material culture, it also changed the landscape. The Weald is an area of south-east England that includes parts of Kent, Hampshire, Surrey and Sussex. Due to the abundance of woodland for making charcoal and the presence of ironstone in the local sandstones, it is an area of Britain that has been producing iron since prehistoric times. Up until the mid-18th century, it produced a large quantity of bar iron and most of the cannons. However, this required a huge amount of charcoal and there is only so much that a coppiced woodland can produce. When the fuel of choice changed to coke, the centre of iron production moved up to the midlands and the Weald was left to recover.

ST DUNSTAN

St Dunstan was an Abbot of Glastonbury Abbey, a Bishop of London and the Archbishop of Canterbury. He had been a blacksmith and it is rumoured that using his red-hot tongs, he grabbed the devil by the nose and shod his cloven hoofs, causing him great pain. He only removed the shoe once the devil promised never to enter a place where a horseshoe hangs over the door. Dunstan was a very popular saint and went a long way to galvanising the reputation of a blacksmith as lucky.

BLACKSMITHING

The term blacksmith comes from the fact that iron is seen as a black metal, due to the fire scale that forms on the surface of the metal during heating. During the Middle Ages, blacksmithing was considered one of the seven mechanical arts along with weaving, war, navigation, agriculture, hunting and medicine. The process must have seemed amazing (as it still does today, I think) with the blacksmith being at the heart of a village community.

As I lit the forge in order to make Ruth some tenterhooks I considered just how many now seemingly incidental artefacts must have been made in forges up and down the country: nails, hinges, pokers, knives, brackets, chains, the list is endless. Tenterhooks, which are used to this day, are small hooked nails upon which wet cloth is hung in order to dry without shrinking after fulling. If you buy material and look at the edge, you will see a series of tiny regularly spaced holes where the tenterhooks have pierced the cloth.

Fiddle, fiddle, fiddle…
Oh, where are you, my
little tenterhook?

I had conferred with Ruth and we had agreed on a size of hook and a volume that needed to be produced. Unlike the majority of blacksmiths today who use coke, Tudor smiths would have used charcoal as their forge fuel. One of the major benefits of charcoal is that it is self-burning, whereas coke will go out. This was quite handy as making tenterhooks was a very fiddly process.

Bending the tenterhook around the anvil

A plethora of tenterhooks ripe for Ruth's cloth

The idea was to draw out the metal and round it into two sharp points, then bend it 90 degrees at around three-quarters of the length. Drawing out means you heat the metal and hit so that it thins and lengthens. This sounds easy except that tenterhooks are somewhere between the size of a nail and the size of a large pin. As the tongs were not small and neither was the hammer, it was a little like performing microsurgery with comically big instruments. Thankfully, the forge was equipped with a couple of small spike anvils dating from the 17th century and they were more conducive to delicate work. There is no set size or shape for an anvil and before iron was mass produced anvils would most likely have been made of stone. I worked with Ian Glasspool, one of the Weald and Downland Museum's volunteers, and together we perfected a little production line. By the end of the day we had enough tenterhooks for Ruth to hang out her material – a tiny window into the way that Tudor industries complemented and relied upon one another.

Tom's Diary

BLACKSMITHING

Although I have extensive experience of working with wood, metalwork was going to be a new skill to acquire. I was more than keen to learn: on my 'Man Plan' of things to do before I'm 40, blacksmithing was definitely in the top five.

All that was required was a forge, an anvil, a hammer and some metal to work. Temperature is all important in blacksmithing and to gauge it, one needs to look at the colour of the metal under heat.

Red metal is metal at 550°C and this stage can be termed 'bending temperature'; 'working temperature' is 750°C and the metal will be orange. Tudor blacksmiths might not have known the exact temperature ranges they were working in but by using the colour as a gauge, they were able to work large or small ingots of pig iron to make a range of tools and utensils. A notable point to make is the delicacy which the craft of blacksmithing sometimes requires. Childhood images of huge men hammering huge bits of metal were quickly replaced as Ruth tasked us with making tenterhooks for her cloth shenanigans.

The blacksmith was a central figure in the urban and rural communities. It was a constantly required skill that also utilised produce from other tradesmen, such as the charcoal burners who provided the fuel for the forge. Sussex in particular had swathes of forest cut down to make charcoal, a lot of which was required by the expanding numbers of blacksmiths in the Tudor age. Training-wise, the apprenticeship for a young blacksmith-to-be was seven years: by the time of completion, the new blacksmith would be skilled enough to start up on his own and if he wanted, take on his own apprentice in a continuing cycle.

LEAD

PETER

Lead ore is often found in association with zinc, silver or copper. The metal, though now known to be hazardous, is relatively easy to extract. It is estimated that at our current rates of consumption, lead supplies will run out in the next 50 years. But this is not the first lead rush we have had. Looking at production rates of lead, the first major peak was 2,000 years ago, when the Romans were generating around 80,000 metric tonnes per year. And the Tudors also found plenty of demand for this highly versatile metal.

The Romans used lead for a number of purposes including lengths of water pipes. However, with the fall of the Roman Empire and the loss of infrastructure, lead production fell off rapidly, reaching a low around AD 850, before climbing to a new high of 90,000 metric tonnes in AD 1750. The Tudor period coincided with this slow but steady increase in the use of and therefore the production of lead. This was particularly prominent in the church. Whenever I think about a church, my mind can't help but recall the lead on the roof, and that which breaks up the stained glass.

Lead cames framing painted glass

Monasteries prior to the dissolution began to invest both time and money into lead mining to provide materials for the surge of church building during the reign of Henry VII. This activity was reflected in the number of candles being used, which implies that many mine shafts were up and running. However, this would prove to be a costly mistake: the availability of what could be termed 'easy lead' was one of the benefits of the dissolution as Henry VIII and Thomas Cromwell stripped out the material for their own purposes.

A later pit head at the ancient lead mine of Snailbeach

SNAILBEACH MINE

When it came to undertaking a project such as digging lead ore out of the ground, smelting it and turning it into a usable metal, we turned to our secret weapon: Colin Richards. We ventured up to Shropshire to Snailbeach, one of the oldest and most prolific lead mines and rumoured to have produced more lead per acre than any other mine in Europe. It is known to date from the Roman period and in 1796, an ingot was found weighing 193 lb and stamped with 'IMP HADRIANI AVG'. The mine fell into disuse but intermittent activity began again in the 12th century with the mine being used again in earnest in 1552.

Colin was armed with a copy of *De Re Metallica* by the German scholar and scientist Georgius Agricola, or Georg Bauer. Published posthumously in 1556, it is the definitive text on mining of the period and remained unsurpassed for a further 180 years. The book covers the pros and cons of mining, how to find veins of ore, how to dig and construct tunnels, the tools and machines required, how to assay the ore prior to crushing, washing and smelting it and how to separate out the various metals.

GOING UNDERGROUND

Reading a book is all well and good, but it never gives you the actual experience. Which is why I found myself descending a ladder into a pit in the ground, armed with chisel and hammer. We set about hammering the earth to break off the ore, silently praying that the whole structure didn't collapse in around our heads. Each time I embark upon a project like this it makes me think about the amount of energy and manpower that goes into producing certain materials and artefacts. When we were satisfied with the amount of ore that we had collected, we brought it back up to the surface in order to try and separate it out from any waste material by smashing it up with hammers. We then set about extracting the metal itself.

In 1554 Burchard Kranich (another German mining engineer) built the first smelt mill for smelting lead in the UK at Makeney, Derbyshire. Prior to this, lead was smelted at sites known as bole hills (sometimes called bail hills). Quite simply, a hearth or a bole was dug on the side of a hill near the top where the wind was strong and provided a natural fanning of the flames. The ore was layered with wood and faggots in a large bonfire which was set alight and burned for around 48 hours. The result was slag, which could then be heated in another furnace to produce molten lead.

Experimental archaeometallurgy – our attempt at making cames

MAKING CAMES

Molten lead can be poured out either into ingots or into moulds to make 'cames': the bars of lead that glass sits in when it is in a window. They are usually either U or H shaped depending on if they are at the base or in the middle of the window and need to take either one or two pieces of glass. This technique was first written about by the Benedictine monk Theophilus Presbyter in the book *De Diversis Artibus* in the first half of the 12th century.

One of the problems with smelting lead is that the metal can evaporate if the fire is too hot, so during the 16th and 17th centuries white coal was used. White coal is wood that has been chopped up and dried over a fire, often in a depression known as a Q-pit. It burns hotter than green wood but not as hot as charcoal; it also has a very low sulphur content and gives quite a good continuous burn.

> **❝ ONE OF THE PROBLEMS WITH SMELTING LEAD IS THAT THE METAL CAN EVAPORATE IF THE FIRE IS TOO HOT ❞**

As always when Colin is involved, we managed to get the desired result. The bole fires were not hugely efficient but any ore that had not turned into slag could be re-fired in the next burn. We certainly got a decent amount of slag, which we then heated and extracted molten lead. We poured out a came and it was amazing to think that this metal had been in the ground only days before. We stood on that hill in Shropshire with the sun setting and breeze encouraging the fire to rage and I thought about how, although the process was scientific, there was a certain amount of mysticism surrounding it. For an outsider who perhaps had only ever toiled in the fields, looking up and seeing these periodically raging fires producing metal must have been quite an experience.

The beautiful material that is freshly poured sheet lead

THE WRITTEN WORD

PETER

With our print media on the decline as we move further into a digital age, it is easy to forget that the written word wasn't always so available. Learning was the preserve of the Church, and a huge part of monastic life was the reading, and reproducing, of manuscripts. Illumination was an art, and the skill we see on existing vellum parchments is astonishing. But in the 15th century, one invention changed all this forever. The printing press meant knowledge no longer had to be copied out by hand or passed down by word of mouth, and ordinary folk could now access what had once been a scholastic arena.

I'm sure the salesman said this was touchscreen!

VELLUM

Vellum is a fine form of parchment. It is made from the skin of an animal, usually calfskin, and like leather it is periodically washed in water and soaked in lime, though unlike leather it is not tanned.

One side of vellum tends to be smoother, with the other side, which is covered in hair, usually rougher. Any scars or nicks that the animal picked up in its life will also show up on the vellum. What's more, if you hold a piece of vellum up to the light, you can usually see the shadow of the backbone of the animal.

The printed word spurred the Reformation

As part of our religious and cultural life, we'd set up a guild – so now we needed a charter. During the early Tudor period these documents were written on vellum. To write on vellum quill pens were used but one disadvantage of a quill pen is the ink will leak out. For this reason the pen has to be held close to the horizontal; scribes who worked on documents used writing slopes that were fairly steep.

A quill pen is a flight feather of a large bird, such as a goose. The nib end has to be sharpened, which is where we get the term penknife from, and the hollow acts as an ink well. The rest of the feather is then surplus to requirement – it looks good, but it does tend to get in the way when writing.

Vellum was (and still is) expensive and writing required a certain amount of planning. It was possible to correct a mistake by taking a sharp knife and scraping off the surface that contained the offending ink but this was obviously something that a scribe would want to avoid. In order to get a straight line, guide lines were marked on the vellum.

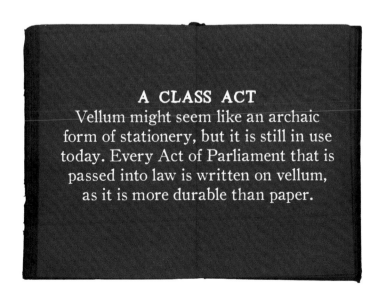

A CLASS ACT
Vellum might seem like an archaic form of stationery, but it is still in use today. Every Act of Parliament that is passed into law is written on vellum, as it is more durable than paper.

THE PRINTING PRESS

However, vellum wasn't the only way of putting pen, or ink, to paper. The idea of printing is an ancient one, with cylinder seals being developed over 5,000 years ago in the Near East. Prior to the printing press, woodblocks were being used. Wood was carved so that the raised areas represented the pictures and text that one wished to transfer to cloth or paper. Ink was applied and the block was stamped onto the page (in some cases the page was rubbed onto the block).

At some point after 1430, Gutenberg developed a process of moveable type printing which he combined with an existing press – one which was probably in use for making wine or cheese. Each metal character was on its own wooden stalk and could be arranged with others to form words and sentences. It is unclear exactly how he constructed his press but his masterpiece, the Gutenberg Bible, still survives. He printed 180 copies of which 48 are still in existence.

Here is information; share it with all. A reconstruction of the first printing press

INKS

The ink used for writing on vellum was a water-based, oak gall ink. This ink was in use during the Roman Empire and only recently went out of production. It was made by boiling iron and galls, found on oak trees and also known as oak apples, in a little water and adding some gum arabic. When used to write on the vellum the ink initially appeared grey in colour but as it dried it darkened to a purplish black.

However, Gutenberg developed a new type of oil-based ink using soot, turpentine (a derivative of the resin in pine trees) and walnut oil. No longer water-based, this meant that books could be printed on both sides of the paper – bringing down the cost of creating a book.

BRITISH BOOKS

The printing industry was brought to Britain by William Caxton, who visited Cologne, set up a press in Bruges, then later established a printing press in Westminster in 1476. *The Canterbury Tales* is considered to be the first book that Caxton printed and over three quarters of the books he published were in English. At the time of the introduction of the printing press, the English language was in a state of flux; the idea of printing started the process of standardising the language.

❝ AT THE TIME OF THE INTRODUCTION OF THE PRINTING PRESS, THE ENGLISH LANGUAGE WAS IN A STATE OF FLUX ❞

We managed to find an old cider press, which we fixed up and used to set our type and press our first pages. For something that looked so crude and simple, it represents an exponential acceleration of society. I wonder out of all the books that were destroyed during the dissolution of the monasteries, how many of them were printed using Gutenberg-style presses? Although the third press in England was set up in a Benedictine monastery in St Albans in 1479, the printing press undoubtedly aided the publication and distribution of the works of the monk Martin Luther, resulting in the Protestant movement in religion and helping bring an end to the monasteries in England.

Print on paper, Dude!
It takes 500 cows to
make a vellum Bible

TUDOR FOOD AND DRINK

Food and drink in Tudor England was very much a celebration of life. The different foods that were on the table were directly linked to the time of year that they were being served and whether or not the household was marking a festival. Sitting at the head of the table in a room where all the estate workers 'knew their place', the yeoman farmer was not only demonstrating how the farm was doing by the produce on the table but also playing a game of politics. A king in his own home, he could curry favour or show disdain, all with a simple meal.

Cooking on wood fires without the taint of coal, the food is so pure and so flavoursome that words fail to emphasise just how vital Tudor meals were. Whether it is mutton spit-roasted over an open wood fire, basted with juices and dredged with herbs, flour and breadcrumbs to form a crust, accompanied by a salad made of edible weeds or a simple meal of bread and cheese, the food and drink of Tudor England rivalled even today's.

THE DIETARY CALENDAR

RUTH

Most of us are aware that fruit and vegetables have a season, even if we are a little hazy on the exact timings. In late 15th- and early 16th-century Britain, meat, fish and dairy produce were also seasonal. The religious calendar of fasting and feasting added another dimension to the yearly round, meaning that food was an ever-changing experience.

Easter, and meat is back on the menu

LATE WINTER

Let's begin our food year at the start of Lent. Forty days before Easter, the garden outside looks bare, ragged and sad. The old woody stalks of cabbages and kale stand battered by the icy winds, sending out hardy little shoots whenever there is a day or two of milder weather. Ragged and well-plundered winter savory hunkers down in one corner, but the rest is bare and half dug over.

The geese are looking thin in the yard and won't lay for another month or two. The cows and sheep are heavy with calves and lambs, eager for any bite of grass or weed they can get, and have to be kept off the precious cabbage shoots.

In the kitchen, the grain ark is half empty but still holds a sack of dried peas and another of dried beans. There's a good stock of oats in the barn and barley, rye and wheat stocks are holding up. High in the

Dried carlin peas are an important Lenten foodstuff

❝ THE COWS AND SHEEP ARE HEAVY WITH CALVES AND LAMBS, EAGER FOR ANY BITE OF GRASS OR WEED THEY CAN GET ❞

A pot of hearty frumenty

rafters hang two rows of salted, dried ling and there is a barrel of pickled herring stood in the corner.

Meanwhile, the Church calendar requires that we eat no meat or eggs or dairy produce. But since the geese are not laying and the cows not milking, it would be grossly uneconomic to kill a beast at this time of year. The rules merely reflect the practical necessity for most of the population: only the wealthy have the wherewithal to break the Church's injunctions.

So what can you cook with these resources? Bread and ale, of course, provide the basic nourishment. Salted ling can be soaked and then stewed with either beans or peas for pottage. Cabbage sprouts at intervals add a little texture and flavour. Peas can be boiled up separately with some winter savory, beaten to a paste in a pestle and mortar and boiled again, pressed in a cloth to make a pease pudding that can be served hot or cold in slices.

Pickled herring can be eaten straight from the barrel with bread. It can also be rinsed off, minced and mixed with coarsely ground oats and a touch of greens, formed into balls and dropped in boiling water for a minute or two. Any of the grains can be made into frumenty by lightly crushing them, swelling them in boiling water and stirring in as much herb as possible (rather like a risotto).

SPRING

Easter is the most important feast of the Christian year. It is a time for celebration, to throw off the dietary restrictions of the past 40 days. Easter also coincides with new supplies. Livestock have begun to give birth, cows and sheep can be milked, and poultry may have begun to lay as the grass springs up to feed them all. Out in the garden, perennial herbs are beginning to show some life and planting can begin in earnest. With milk in abundance over the next few months, a housewife needs to prepare for cheese making so that the bounty does not go to waste. In order to do that, she has to select a young animal to slaughter for its rennet producing stomach. This in turn supplies the iconic dish of Easter Sunday – veal. This will be the first meat that anyone has eaten since early February, and probably the first fresh meat since Christmas.

> ❝ OUT IN THE GARDEN, PERENNIAL HERBS ARE BEGINNING TO SHOW SOME LIFE AND PLANTING CAN BEGIN IN EARNEST ❞

The milk and cream that now floods in can be eaten and drunk alone or turned into rich thick creamy frumenty, baked into custard or used to poach the remaining veal. On Wednesdays, Fridays and Saturdays no meat can be eaten, but dairy produce is allowed so the salt ling can now be soaked and poached in milk, or fried in homemade butter. Omelette-like 'fraises', thickened with breadcrumbs, make good portable meals out in the fields. Stillborn lambs provide bursts of meat eating in April, flavoured with the newly sprung herbs in the garden and hedgerows. Supplies of dried peas and beans however are getting very low.

SUMMER

June sees the height of egg laying and butter and cheese production with green leafy vegetables such as orach, spinach, Good King Henry and fat hen making an appearance. The price of beef is beginning to fall and fresh eels are the most available fish. For those with land and money, dishes of cream cheese and raspberries, strawberries and cream complement good roast beef.

Spring salads of edible weeds made a welcome change

Mutton is the meat of high summer, as flocks are thinned of the old and unprofitable after the fleeces have been shorn. Poultry, too, makes it to the table as chicks, goslings and ducklings have been raised and plentiful grass and weeds have fattened them. Mackerel is plentiful and cheap at this time of year, with salmon and trout available to those who can afford it or own the fishing rights. In the dairy, production shifts from the sweet butter and soft cheeses of the spring to salted butter and harder cheese, intended to provide stores for thinner times. Gardens are in full swing and the first root vegetables join the leafy greens in the kitchen. Dishes of fresh green peas poached in cream accompany roast and boiled mutton with green herb sauce; cheese cakes give way to grass-fed roast goose.

> **" SUMMER, PARADOXICALLY, IS THE TIME OF YEAR WHEN THE POOR GO HUNGRIEST "**

An abundant pea and bean crop was especially welcome in the cottage closes of the poorer sort

Meals were generally simple but ever-changing as the seasons turned

LATE SUMMER AND AUTUMN

August and September are times of hard work and plenty of food. Egg production is falling off but as each successive variety of grain harvest arrives in the barn, pies, pastries and 'bready' cakes come to the fore. Beef is at its best and its cheapest and the ale flows. Preparing for the winter months ahead, stocks of pickled and smoked herring are bought at market whilst they too are abundant, and the loft begins to fill with hard rounds of cheese. Onions from the garden are boiled whole as a vegetable or minced and served with liver, kidneys and other offal. Joints of brisket are boiled and served alongside pottages of ox tail and young turnip. Pies and pasties are carried to the fields.

> ❝ ONIONS FROM THE GARDEN ARE BOILED WHOLE AS A VEGETABLE, OR MINCED AND SERVED WITH LIVER, KIDNEYS AND OTHER OFFAL ❞

November is the usual time for slaughtering and processing a pig or two, making sausages, hams and bacon, enjoying the offal fresh and sousing (or pickling) collar joints. Salt cod is purchased to add to the store and the cows are finally allowed to run dry, preserving their strength for the hard winter to come. With milk and eggs off the menu and the garden reduced to cabbages and root vegetables, hearty pottages thick with grain and animal fats become the seasonal flavour.

CHRISTMAS

Advent is the second great fast of the religious cycle, requiring four weeks of abstinence from meat (though eggs and dairy produce are allowed if you still have them). The stored herring come to the fore, along with fresh cod and most of the flat fish if you can get them. Turnips, parsnips, skirrets and carrots add variety and bulk to the pottage. With stored salt butter still on the menu, pastry is good food in Advent: it can be wrapped around fish, made into little bite sized honey and breadcrumb stuffed 'farts', or eaten on its own, deep fat fried and with a scrape of sugar.

Christmas offers the first meat eating day of celebration. Pig's head was our traditional dish: not a fresh one, but pickled or soused into a form of brawn some weeks previously, stored through Advent and brought out to be boiled, decorated, sung about and eaten on Christmas day. Mince pies of mixed meats, suet and dried fruit were shaped to resemble the manger that Jesus was placed in at birth. Twelve days later, it was time for a great cake of the finest bread dough, enriched with as much butter and cream as you could muster, scattered throughout with exotic dried fruit and spices and baked in as large a single lump as your oven would take.

After the celebrations, cold January was a time for living upon the stores you had laid in – the hard rounds of cheese, the bacon and hams – till Lent began the cycle again.

I didn't spend a lot of time on elaborate cooking. Fresh, quality ingredients, simply prepared, still provided delicious fare, although it was rarely photogenic. I wish I could let you taste and smell it yourself

Tom's Diary

FOOD

Food in its basest form is fuel. Working as a Tudor farmer means long days and strenuous physical work that takes its toll on the body and a high-calorie diet is vital to keep going.

However, one of the great pleasures in life is sitting with friends enjoying some food and a few drinks. There is something slightly surreal about doing that in a Tudor style – surreal simply because it is so similar to the modern day. We eat the same things, such as bread and cheese. We drink beer. We sit and talk about the same things: work, the weather (sadly closely integrated to the majority of our work on the Tudor farm) and what we'll do when we finally get some free time.

If I relate Tudor food to the modern day in this instance then the word to use is 'organic'. We made what we ate and it was a great aspect to our Tudor farm experience. In a period without TV or radio, food might have been fuel, but the meal itself was a welcome social event. And personally, I can always find time in my life for bread, cheese and ale!

BREAD

RUTH

 **B**efore potatoes, rice and pasta became part of the national diet, bread formed the basic staple food for everyone in Britain. From the highest to the lowest in the land, bread was eaten at every meal and it provided the vast majority of the calories consumed within the country.

Bread was the most important foodstuff of all

The bread consumed was not always the same, however. Bread made exclusively from wheat flour was in the minority and regarded as something of a luxury product. This came in several grades, from small white rolls to large brown loaves, weighing up to four pounds. The rolls were raised with fresh yeast drawn from the ale brewing vats, while the large loaves combined wholegrain wheat with added bran, and were raised with sourdough stored from the previous batch, rather than fresh yeast.

> **❝ MIXES OF GRAINS PROVIDED BREADS THAT REFLECTED DIFFERENT PRICES, DIFFERENT DESIRED FLAVOURS, AND DIFFERENT LOCAL GROWING CONDITIONS ❞**

Beyond the privileged world of pure wheaten bread, barley was the dominant grain. Barley was cheaper than wheat, but more expensive than oats and rye, and these grains were also important. Mixes of grains provided breads that reflected different prices, different desired flavours, and different local growing conditions. Upland areas of the country struggled to ripen wheat, and in bad years even barley crops failed on the hills. By contrast, the hardier rye and oats could be relied upon. Many farmers grew different grains as a mixed crop in the field: 'maslin' was the name for a

Top: Ale barm – fresh yeast from the top of the ale brewing vat
Bottom: Sourdough – a piece of yeast-filled dough

Bread for sale had to comply with a range of strict regulations

wheat and rye mix and 'dredge' was oats and barley. Flour for bread could even include ingredients that were not grains at all. Peas and beans could be dried and ground up, and in times of famine, acorns were sometimes added.

THE PRICE OF A LOAF OF BREAD

Prices for commercially baked bread were fixed by law. This was the very first foodstuff to be subject to state regulation, and an attempt to protect consumers and give a degree of food security to the population at large. Loaves had to be sold at a fixed price – generally a penny a loaf – with the size and weight set at the county assizes to reflect the availability and price of flour: in a year of abundant harvests, the penny loaf was substantially larger than the loaf from a year of scarcity. Officials checked the weight and quality of loaves on sale at market and penalties for infringements were swift and stern. A 'baker's dozen' became established as 13 rolls rather than 12 as the baking trade sought to protect itself against accidental short measures and the public punishment in the town stocks that they could bring.

> ❝ OFFICIALS CHECKED THE QUALITY OF LOAVES ON SALE AT MARKET AND PENALTIES FOR INFRINGEMENTS WERE SWIFT AND STERN ❞

A clean, swept oven at the end of the day

Even in the countryside, many people bought rather than baked their own bread. Not everyone had an oven and even for smaller households that did, it wasn't always sensible to light it on economic grounds. Sourcing the fuel to fire an oven might be relatively simple if you had a large farm at your disposal, but for those with small plots, wood could be hard to come by. Some villages shared a communal oven with each resident taking a turn at providing the fuel and firing the oven, into which everyone else would put their loaves. In most cases, however, one person took over and charged a small fee for the service – becoming, in effect, a commercial baker. As in the nursery rhyme, the villagers would 'pat it and prick it and mark it with B', in order to keep track of which loaves were theirs.

A SLICE OF LANGUAGE

Bread has been a staple of human existence for over 30,000 years. In terms of a monastic community it is with communion bread that a fast is broken which is where we get the term break-fast. Stale bread known as a trencher measuring 6 inches by 4 inches was often used as a plate and may be the origin of 'a square meal'.

We are used to slicing our bread vertically but in the Tudor period bread, was sliced horizontally. The base of the loaf was contaminated with the ash and the small embers of the bread oven so the better part of the bread was the upper crust. This is where we get the modern-day term, as the more important people at the dining table were given the 'upper crust' of the bread.

While baking at home was considered to be women's work, commercial baking was generally done by men. Monks generally hired a professional baker to produce their daily bread within the grounds of the monastery, although there were occasions when they bought in additional loaves from outside the walls. The baker hired his own helpers, recruiting heavily from his own family. Occasionally, wives and widows are listed separately in the monastery accounts, receiving wages for their work in the bakery.

WHAT DID TUDOR BREAD TASTE LIKE?

The bread that was produced in Tudor times was markedly different to that sold in 21st-century supermarkets. Grain was grown in 1500 was much lower in gluten, so could not produce the soft and fluffy texture that we are accustomed to. The ovens gave the bread a strong crust and Tudor wheat baked up into fairly solid, dense loaves, with the other grains producing even heavier bread. Tudor bread was filling, chewy and came in many different forms: the mixture of grains and raising agents meant that flavours varied a great deal.

> ❝ TUDOR BREAD WAS FILLING, CHEWY AND CAME IN MANY DIFFERENT FORMS ❞

Ale-barm-raised maslin bread, with its mixture of wheat and rye, formed our usual household bread

I have both made and eaten lots of bread of these types. Bread made of dredge (oats and barley) and raised with sourdough has an almost sweet taste to it, alongside the sour note from the raising agent. It can be a little doughy in texture but keeps well and is excellent eaten with soups and stews – the 'pottage' that formed such a major part of working people's diet. Maslin bread, made from wheat and rye, is pale in colour, more grainy and open in texture. It is the wheat flavour that is most pronounced in this type of loaf. I liked it on its own with a scrape of butter.

The bread of poverty and scarcity was a mixture of whatever grain could be got. It often consisted largely of the bran that had been sifted out of the whiter bread of the better off and mixed with ground dried peas and beans. It is fairly unpleasant stuff. The pea and bean flour has a rank taste and the bran makes it very scratchy and chewy in texture. It doesn't hold together very well, cracking and crumbling apart. It also provides less nutrition than bread made with 'better' flour.

MONKS' BREAD

Although we had looked at domestic bread production, we were also interested in the daily grind of a monk's life – a grind fuelled on two pounds of bread per monk per day. That meant a monastery kitchen had to produce huge quantities of bread on a daily basis, so how did they go about doing this?

Someone who knows all about making bread is David Carter. I met David in the kitchen at Cowdray Park, the neighbouring Tudor period house to our farm. The kitchen was built in a separate building from the house so that if it caught fire it wouldn't burn down. In fact, the opposite ended up happening: the house caught fire and burnt down, while the kitchen survived.

David had researched the bread that would have been produced in that kitchen and had come up with three main elements. Firstly, the monks would have been making the hosts for the Eucharist. These were made of an unleavened bread and were quite large, certainly larger than they are now, so that they could be seen by the lay congregation through the rood screen of a church. The kitchen also produced bread for the monks' table and bread that may have been used in the mass as a panis benedictus (bread that is blessed by the priest but isn't consecrated). There were two types of this table bread: the run of the mill bread made from wheat flour, barley flour and rye flour; and the white bread for the abbot that was made from fine white flour that had to be sieved by passing it through a bolt of cloth.

David Carter: master baker extraordinaire

To make the bread for the monks' table, we combined the flour in a bowl and mixed it thoroughly with our hands along with some salt. Salt is the magic ingredient that activates the yeast. The salt must be fine rather than rock salt, otherwise you tend to get salt crystals in the bread. We then made a well and added our water; to this we poured in our yeast.

The yeast David had made was a sourdough one. This simply meant he took some flour and some water, mixed them together and then put them in a warm place. This ferments over a few days and can be fed further water and flour as it activates. The sourdough yeast was actually trying to escape from its container as we poured it into the water in our well of flour. The yeast

Peter mixing the sourdough
prior to kneading it

" THE SOURDOUGH YEAST WAS ACTUALLY TRYING TO ESCAPE FROM ITS CONTAINER AS WE POURED IT "

was very bitter with an almost cheesy, vinegary taste. We mixed this yeast with the water and then gradually began to mix in the flour. As if by magic, the contents of the bowl went from looking like a bowl of water to looking like a large round of dough. We then had to knead this dough.

One mistake that people sometimes make is to put flour on the board but that introduces raw flour to the mix: David explained you have to wet the board with water and do the same with your hands. We then spread the dough and starting at one end, systematically pulled and kneaded the dough until it was balled up again. We repeated this until the dough started fighting back: this signified that the yeast had lined up and the bread was ready to be popped in a bowl to prove. While the dough was proving we worked on the abbot's bread. This was the same, except the yeast was a beer barm – the foam that beer produces when it is fermenting.

When our sourdough was ready, we liberally dusted our board with flour and turned it out. It had doubled in size. We now had to knock it back which we did by squashing it and folding it in on itself. We then turned it over and David scored the waist of the bread with a knife to form the trencher. He scored the top so that as the bread rose while it baked, it would have room to expand. We then popped it in our bread oven to bake.

When we opened up the oven just over an hour later the smell was amazing. David leaned in and pulled out the perfect loaves. It was moments like these that I felt like I'd gone back in time to an early Tudor monastery.

A sourdough loaf that
was as good as it looked

BAKING AT HOME

RUTH

Ovens of grander establishments were often an integral aspect of the structure of the house, forming part of the stone walls of the chimney. Our home, however, was timber framed and without a chimney, and so our oven was a free-standing structure built in the corner of the kitchen. It stood on a stone base and was waist high and circular with an ash hole at the front. On top of this was the dome of the oven, brick built and insulated with a layer of daub. The smoke from our fires wound its way up to the roof and out between the eaves and the tiles, cooling as it went.

To use the oven, I needed to build a fire inside it and heat up the bricks of the dome. Small twiggy bits of wood are best for this, as they release their energy quicker than the slow burn of large logs. People living near heath land used broom, gorse bushes or old heather. Our farm was in the Weald where wood is plentiful, so my fuel came from coppicing.

MAKING THE DOUGH

Our usual bread was maslin bread, made with around 60% wheat flour and 40% rye flour. While I would sift the bran out to make cake and pastry, for the bread I left it in. The yeast, meanwhile, came from the froth that rose on our ale when I was brewing. The process began in the afternoon of the

FIREWOOD

The wood used in ovens was known as 'faggots'. These were the brash (foliage, small branches) that were cut off the poles and timber and bundled together. Poles, timber and faggots could all be purchased from those who owned or managed woodland commercially. Legislation defined the size of poles and faggots, designating the lengths and circumferences of the bundles.

We still have some examples of surviving Tudor firewood today. When Henry VIII's flagship, the *Mary Rose*, sank just outside Portsmouth Harbour, she had been provisioned for duty. Archaeologists recovering the wreckage discovered, along with many other exciting finds, seven hundred pieces of firewood stacked close by the galley, or kitchen area, of the ship. All of the pieces corresponded exactly to the legal firewood standards of the day.

Like most ordinary folk, we had no chimney, cooking instead on an open hearth, with a free-standing oven to the side of the room

Ale barm and water was poured into a well in the flour

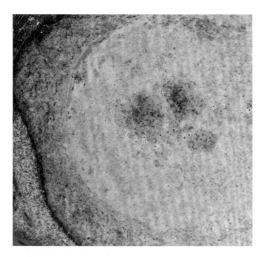

day before I fired the oven. I measured out my flour into the dough trough: two of my wooden scoops for a loaf along with a large handful of salt for the whole batch. I then fetched a small jug of ale froth, which I mixed with a large jug of water.

All weights and measures in the kitchen were judged by eye and experience, not by scales and numbers. You soon get a feel for how full a jug or bowl should be when you are regularly cooking the same recipe. The froth and water were poured into a large well in the flour; at this stage it was best to err on the side of too wet rather than too dry. I then scuffed some of the surrounding flour over the top of the liquid and left the trough for an hour or two. Before I went to bed, I stirred the flour and liquid together and left it once more. The following morning, the yeast had had time to grow throughout the mass. The slow cool fermentation had begun to change the flour, releasing the gluten and allowing flavours to develop. The overnight rising helps reduce the kneading work and brings the dough to a soft elastic consistency much quicker than a fast warm rise would produce.

KNEADING TIME

In the afternoon, I began the business of kneading the dough. Working such large quantities calls for a little ingenuity. It is perfectly possible to just divide it up and

Kneading the dough by hand rather than foot

hand knead each lump, but much quicker and easier to use a 'brake'. This is a piece of wood, rather like a heavy rolling pin, that is attached to a table with a leather hinge. Taking hold of one end of the brake, you can bash up and down whilst you feed the dough through, turning and folding it as you go. If you didn't have a brake, another alternative was to knead the dough with your feet. Here,

you wrap the mass up securely in a large floured cloth and lay it on the floor. Then you take off your shoes, wash your feet and begin to tread the dough. The foot method is certainly effective and less exhausting, but I found that getting the dough off the cloth can sometimes be very troublesome. If the batch is perfect, it does release in a single lump; the merest hint of too much water, however, and you have problems.

BAKING THE BREAD

Once the kneading is complete, it is time to shape the loaves and light the oven. The simplest, most labour saving method is to take a faggot and prop it up with one end in the fire. Once it is burning merrily, you can pick it up and transfer it into the oven. When that faggot is burning along its complete length, another can be added into the oven.

Our oven took five faggots to bring it up to bread baking heat if it was cold, but only four if it had been in use the previous day. All ovens are a little different, and it can take a few experiments to achieve the perfect burn. As you watch the fire burn, it is important to keep a close eye on it and adjust the rate that you add fuel and the flow of oxygen into the fire. The aim is for large slow arabesques of pale yellow flame caressing the whole inner surface of the oven. Too much fuel at once drops the temperature inside the fire; if the fire takes hold at the mouth of the oven, it can leave the back of the oven oxygen depleted, preventing the fuel behind from burning.

It takes around 45 minutes of a good burn to get the oven up to heat. The shape and colour of the fire gives you a clue when the temperature has been achieved, as will a handful of fine flour thrown against the back wall, which should spark when it touches the wall. The embers must now be raked out quickly onto the floor and scraped back, out of the way into the ash hole. A wet mop is run around the base of the oven to roughly clean it and to introduce a touch of steam. The loaves can now be slid into the oven, in the space where the fire was only a minute ago. The door is then propped in place and any gaps sealed with a smear of flour and water paste.

Forty minutes later, it is time to crack the seal and open the door: the bread is done (you can check this by tapping their bases – if they are cooked the loaf will sound hollow). The oven will have dropped to the perfect temperature to cook a batch of small pies and tarts, so make sure you have them ready prepared to pop in and make the most of that precious baking heat. These loaves have a good solid crust, keep well, and above all, smell and taste fantastic.

ALE & OTHER DRINKS

RUTH

A fter bread, ale was the second most important source of calories in most people's diets. It also provided a large array of trace minerals and vitamins. In conjunction with mixed grain bread, ale could supply almost all that a person needs for healthy living, with the notable exception of vitamin C. Ale therefore should be seen, not as a luxury, but as a necessity and perhaps more as a foodstuff than as a drink.

It was ale, rather than beer that was generally drunk in Britain at this time. The technical difference between the two being hops: beer is flavoured with, and preserved by the hop plant, while ale is not. Without the preservative nature of hops, ale goes off quite quickly, within five to ten days according to weather and storage conditions. As a result, it has to be brewed regularly in smallish quantities. It can however be flavoured with a huge variety of herbs from heather to sage, nettles to ale cost (a plant whose common name reflects its most usual use). Hops have a bitter flavour, and without them ale is a much sweeter drink: it can be thick and nutty, or light and flowery depending not only upon the herb flavourings but also upon details of the brewing process.

WILD YEASTS
One of the main ingredients of ale was yeast. This too was an area of experimentation. Wild yeasts are present in the air and upon both grains and fruits naturally in the countryside. Those that grow upon the skins of fruit make the best wines and those that grow upon the surfaces of grains and seeds make the best ale and beer. Yeasts varied radically from one farmhouse to the next, with a different blend of wild yeasts present in each imparting quite different flavours to both the bread and the ale. A reputation as a good brewster might well come down to the strain of yeast that you had access to.

Brewing was a feminine task

For a monastery, brewing was a large undertaking

Most ale was brewed by women as part of their domestic routine, providing for their families. Pubs, or alehouses, were also run and supplied by women, often those older and poorer who could not manage the labour of farming. Indeed, the name Brewster, meaning a woman who brews, is older than the name Brewer, meaning a man who brews. They stuck a bush on a pole out of the window of their homes as a signal that they had ale for sale, both for people to take away or consume sitting on a bench outside. A licence was needed for this, with a promise to keep strict moral control around their premises and prevent idle 'tippling'.

❝ THEY STUCK A BUSH ON A POLE OUT OF THE WINDOW OF THEIR HOMES AS A SIGNAL THAT THEY HAD ALE FOR SALE ❞

Abbeys in 1500 were one of the very few places where you found men in charge of this feminine skill. Even here, though, much of the actual work was done by the wives and daughters of those with the official title. Abbeys were also among the first places where beer rather than ale was brewed. The enormous quantities involved encouraged investment in large vats,

Barley, the raw ingredient of ale

Spreading the barley

tubs and barrels. With large stone cellars available, it began to be more useful to brew long-keeping beer. Even so, many monks, as with laymen, continued to prefer the sweeter ale that they were accustomed to, rather than the bitter beer that was more popular on the continent.

BREWING ALE

The basic raw ingredient of ale is traditionally barley, although you can make ale and beer out of any grain. The barley is malted to convert its starch content into the natural sugars that will feed the yeast. This is achieved by allowing the grains to sprout and then stopping the process before the sugars can be utilised by the growing shoot. Getting the process just right was something of a challenge, but rather fun. The barley is winnowed and sifted to clean all the weed seed from it and then spread out on a clean wooden floor to an even depth, around an inch deep, and water is sprinkled on. The grain is stirred about and watered until the grains are all equally damp and re-spread out this time to a thicker depth of three or four inches. A few hours later, the process is repeated to encourage each grain to absorb just enough water to germinate. Stirring, watering and re-spreading continues at intervals until all the grains have swelled. Now the pile of grain is concentrated into an even depth of six to eight inches to allow a little warmth to build.

Watering the malt

Over the next few days the heap needs to be regularly stirred in order to give each grain a turn in the warm, moist middle of the mass. In cold weather the heap is deepened in order to keep up the temperature; in warm weather it is spread out. With both warmth and water the grains prepare to sprout, making that all-important transformation from starch to sugar. Careful management of the heap ensures that all the grain is ready at the same moment. We had a few worried moments when the centre of the pile started to sprout whilst the edges remained stubbornly lifeless. Some frantic, overdue stirring more or less solved the problem, but the ale made from that batch of grain was undoubtedly thinner and weaker than our better ones.

> **WE HAD A FEW WORRIED MOMENTS WHEN THE CENTRE OF THE PILE STARTED TO SPROUT WHILST THE EDGES REMAINED STUBBORNLY LIFELESS**

When the seed coats begin to split and the first pale tips of the new shoots appear, the grain must be moved from the malting floor to the kiln for a blast of even heat that kills the shoots but doesn't scorch the grain. The best malting kilns were purpose-built structures with low arches, beneath which a fire could be lit, and a smooth plastered surface on top where the grain could be spread. Many people managed by using the floor of their ovens, spreading a layer

My wild captured yeast

of malt inside after they had finished the weekly bake. For small regular batches an oven is sufficient, but if you had to render a proportion of your rent in malted barley (as was often the case for abbey-owned farms), the malting kiln was essential.

The other main ingredient of ale is yeast. Capturing those yeasts and putting them to work is simple, if a little haphazard. Just take a large handful of coarsely crushed grain, add some warm water to make a thick sloppy 'gloop' and stand it outside, away from obvious sources of pollution but near to a grain field. Sometimes the mixture will simply go mouldy, but usually you will see signs of fermentation indicating that you have been successful.

> ❝ MANY A YOUNG WOMAN EMBARKING UPON MARRIAGE TOOK A LUMP OF OLD DOUGH AND A POT OF FROTHY ALE FROM HER FAMILY HOME WITH HER TO START HER OWN HOUSEKEEPING ROUTINES ❞

Next, you need to clean your yeast from any mould or filth. This is a matter of skimming off any frothy matter and adding it to a bowl of new clean flour and water, standing it somewhere warm and clean and allowing the yeasts to multiply. You may have to repeat the process several times to completely clean it. Once you have a good culture it is best to keep it alive, reserving a little from each brew or bake for use next time. Many a young woman embarking upon marriage took a lump of old dough and a pot of frothy ale from her family home with her to start her own housekeeping routines.

THE BREWING BEGINS

With malt and yeast at hand the actual brewing can start. Water is brought to the boil (sterilising it and making ale and beer a much safer option than plain water) and poured onto a measure of malt in a wooden tub. This is a good moment to add flavoursome herbs. I couldn't get any heather (a flavour that I really like) but there was no shortage of other types to try. The tub

Der Bierbreuwer.

A German commercial brewhouse, where beer rather than ale predominated – an ancestor of modern commercial beer

is then covered and wrapped around with a woollen blanket if the weather is cold, as you try to keep the water hot as it leaches the sugars out of the malted barley. The resultant thick, dark lukewarm liquid is drawn off into a new tub and for economy's sake, a second batch of water is poured onto the malt to make a weaker, less alcoholic ale (small ale). The jug of frothy yeast is added to the original liquor and once again the lid and blanket go on. The ale is left to brew overnight.

The first job of the next day in the brewhouse is to collect a new jug of frothy yeast from the top of the vat. In Germany they used the yeasts that fell to the bottom of the vat and formed a sludge beneath the ale: we traditionally used the yeasts that rose to the surface. With the new yeast put to one side, the new ale can be strained off into pots or barrels with almost airtight lids to store it. The 'almost airtight' is important: fermentation will continue more slowly for a while and the resultant gases must be able to escape whilst dirt and flies must be kept out.

Of all the batches of ale that I have made, my favourite was a small ale flavoured with elderflower. Peter and Tom preferred some of the thicker, stronger brews.

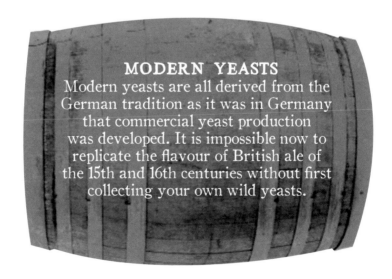

MODERN YEASTS
Modern yeasts are all derived from the German tradition as it was in Germany that commercial yeast production was developed. It is impossible now to replicate the flavour of British ale of the 15th and 16th centuries without first collecting your own wild yeasts.

MEAD

Mead is a drink made from fermenting honey in water and then flavoured with a variety of ingredients. It was drunk in monastic communities on feast days, especially prior to the Norman Conquest, but its popularity waned as wine became more readily available. It is one of the oldest alcoholic drinks and is relatively simple to make. At its very basic level mead is just honey mixed with hot water that has been boiled at a ratio of one to four, with any scum being removed. The mixture is shaken up before yeast is added: I imagine the yeast used may have been a sourdough yeast or a beer barm. To flavour the yeast it is simply a case of adding other ingredients. It takes a couple of months to ferment before all activity stops and it can be racked or bottled.

The anthropologist Lévi-Strauss viewed mead as a cultural milestone and our progression as a race from living within nature to living within society. Mead is certainly entwined within the folklore of various societies: in Norse mythology the Poetic Mead is a drink said to inspire artistic flair and allow the drinker to become like a scholar. Those drinking it will have an unsurpassed depth of knowledge and be able to answer any question (there is many a pub in Britain where you might be mistaken to think that the inhabitants have had a fair old dose of mead themselves!).

> **❝ THOSE DRINKING IT WILL HAVE AN UNSURPASSED DEPTH OF KNOWLEDGE AND BE ABLE TO ANSWER ANY QUESTION ❞**

Perhaps more importantly, mead represents our relationship with the honeybee. Bees are essential to farming and the pollination of plants: a large proportion of the food that we eat as a global race is dependent on their survival. Although bees are 'farmed' they are still wild and have been around for about a million years. Prior to the evolution of hives that had removable combs in the 19th century and the development of centrifugal honey extractors, honey was extracted from wax by pressing it. Although this manages to get most of the honey out, it doesn't get all of it. To clean the expensive wax prior to making candles, the chances are it was washed with warm water and that is the start of your mead. As a large source of wax was quite important for monasteries, I imagine that is why mead continued to be made.

I remember the first time I ever tried mead. It was at Buckfast Abbey in Devon and I had been told that mead was a truly terrible drink. However, I remember it being extremely nice (although I do have a sweet tooth).

A monk placing a skep in a bee bole

MEAD AND HONEYMOONS

Although the etymology of the term honeymoon is uncertain, one suggestion is that it originated from the idea that a newly married couple should drink honey mead for the duration of one moon in order to improve fertility.

Tom's Diary

MALTING BARLEY

The ale of the Tudor period was a different beast to more modern day beers. It provided Tudor workers with a safer option to water for hydration during the working day and its low alcohol content allowed the farmers to continue to work from dawn to dusk. It was a privilege to help Ruth with the malting process, a domain usually occupied solely by women.

The malting process was both scientific and very intuitive, with attention to detail being key. Strangely enough, the process of piling up the barley, saturating it, raking it out and repeating this procedure was extremely therapeutic and a very nice contrast to wrestling animals and building 'stuff' out of wood.

The barley was an assault on the senses: visually it looked amazing but the smell as the barley began to soak up water and subsequently started to germinate was incredible. It is hard to relate the smell to anything else, but if anything it smelt healthy (a strange observation when one is making beer). The malting process is not an arduous task and in fact it is quite satisfying. The making of ale provided enough calories to the working man to allow him to work on the big tasks and was thus a crucial part of Tudor life. The only times we drank ale were either social or at work when it felt well-earned!

SALT

alt has long been essential to human existence. While there are only five distinct tastes – bitterness, sourness, sweetness, umami and saltiness – none has had such a profound importance to society as salt. It has been used as a preservative, as a flavour enhancer, as a medicine and it can even be used as a weapon to spoil agricultural ground. During Tudor times salt was very much a prized and expensive item, both for the flavour it afforded and the valuable ability to salt and preserve foods.

Salt in a salt – pride of place in a household

Salt was so highly valued that it would be placed in a container known as a salt, which were often ornately decorated. They always had lids to reiterate how precious the contents were. This salt would then be placed at the centre of the top table in the communal dining hall and acted very much as a status symbol: if you had salt, you had money. Houses were even built with a nook in the chimney known as a salt hole as this was a good place to keep your salt and stop it getting 'claggy' with the moisture in the air.

" IF YOU HAD SALT, YOU HAD MONEY "

Part of the reason that salt was so expensive (in comparison to today) was because it was taxed in other countries, increasing the export costs, and the quantities that were needed were vast. Fish farming was a booming industry in Tudor England and there was an increase in seagoing fishing vessels. All the fish had to be preserved and the best way to do this was to salt them. After the Reformation Henry VIII persisted with abstaining from meat, as this was a good way to keep the demand for fish up. Then there

Who will buy my salty butter?

was butter: if the recipe laid down by the Bishop of Winchester in 1305 was still followed in the monasteries, then they too would have been using an immense amount of salt in their butter production. His recipe calls for one pound of salt to every ten pounds of butter, which is 10%: salted butter that we buy in shops is normally around 2%.

MARTINMAS

Martinmas (10th November) celebrated St Martin, an austere Roman soldier who had converted to Christianity, and was the day that many animals were slaughtered. This served two purposes. It took the strain off of the farms in trying to keep alive large animal stocks and it ensured a good source of meat throughout the winter months. However, to keep this meat it had to be salted (even if you intend to smoke meat you need to salt it first).

MAKING SALT

Beneath the ground in Cheshire and Worcestershire lies a large deposit of rock salt, left from a long dried up ancient sea. Ground water rising as springs in this area emerge, not as fresh water, but salty, having dissolved the rock through which it has passed. This was a major source of salt in medieval and Tudor Britain.

Sea salt, produced by the action of the sun upon sea water in organised shallow pans, had been important in the fenlands of Norfolk and Lincolnshire in earlier times, but harsh economics and rising sea levels had severely diminished this part of the salt industry in Britain by 1500. Imported salt from warmer shores formed the majority of salt supplies for those in London and along the south coast.

> **" SALT SUPPLIES COULD FORM ONE OF A HOUSEHOLD'S MAJOR EXPENSES "**

The home grown salt industry was concentrated around the town of Nantwich, where streams were deliberately diverted to run through salt rock, the waters collected and boiled up in large flat pans to evaporate off the water, leaving salt crystals behind to be gathered and packed into baskets for transport and sale all over the country.

Salt was one of the staples of life, permitting meat, fish and cheese to be stored throughout the damp Northern European winter. Smoked foods in our climate also need to be lightly salted before being hung in the smoke. In drier climes it is possible to preserve meats and fish by air drying and to smoke fatty foods with no other help, but in our part of the world we need salt to keep the bacteria at bay.

Salt supplies could form one of a household's major expenses because it formed one of the few bulk ingredients that had to be bought in, rather than being sourced upon a

Salt was a cash commodity

*Smoked meat and fish required
a preliminary salting*

household's own holding. Salt was very much a cash economy commodity, unlike, say, carrots.

Cheshire salt, having to be transported overland upon trains of pack horses, was no cheaper in our corner of the land than that imported from France and Spain. However many of the salt or 'wich' houses of Cheshire were in monastic hands, a fact which may well have influenced the provisioning of sister houses to the south.

All around the salt towns, but never within them due to the problems of pollution, were 'walling lands', yards or areas set out with furnaces, sheds and wood stores. Owned largely by the gentry and the monasteries, workers rented the rights to use them along with carefully regulated access to the brine pits to gather the salty water.

Upon the furnaces stood salt pans, a yard wide, two yards long and about a foot deep formed of lead upon a wooden frame. Lead is a soft metal, unable to support the weight of such a volume of water spread across such a large surface area by itself, so these pans had a system of wooden struts and iron hooks that held up the base of the pan, transferring the weight to an overarching wooden frame held clear of the flames.

Producing salt from naturally occuring brine springs was an important industry around Nantwich

The brine was ladled into the pans and the furnaces beneath were fired with wood that was coppiced on the surrounding hillsides. As the brine began to boil, the salt workers or 'wallers' removed the dirt and other impurities by throwing in proteins. Ox blood was the cheapest available such protein. It rose to the surface as it cooked binding all the unwanted matter into a solid frothy scum that could be easily skimmed off the surface.

When sufficient water had evaporated to leave a grainy semi-solid mixture in the pan conical wicker baskets were placed over the pan and the wet salty mass was shovelled in and allowed to drain back into the remaining brine. Once the cones were full of drained salt they were stacked alongside the furnaces and allowed to dry out fully, before being loaded, still in their conical baskets onto the back of the pack horses.

The wicker wrapped cones of salt available to the rest of us at market were solid lumps. Free running, granular salt that we are accustomed to purchasing in the 21st century is the result of a process and additive invented in the mid-19th century. The Tudor housewife had to chip bits off her salt block. But she did have the choice of many types and grades of salt.

A WOMAN'S WORK

The 'wallers' of Cheshire at this time are recorded as being mostly women, their husbands being more occupied in agriculture or employed in other crafts. Perhaps the lifting and shifting of water, and the tending of huge pans over fires fitted closely with contemporary ideas of women's work, although it was probably a simple mixture of low profit margins and the possibility of combining such work with childcare responsibilities that encouraged families to adopt a strategy in which women carried on the trade whilst men pursued more financially rewarding work elsewhere.

A salt block – housewives would
chip off what was needed

Prices varied according to the 'whiteness', or purity, of the salt, whether it was rock salt or sea salt, its region of origin and the size of the crystals. Each type had its uses, some being suited best to fish preservation (large rough crystals), some for brine to salt beef (mid-range rock salt); the whitest salt was chosen for cheese, whilst household cleaning was not only cheapest with dark grey rock salt, but also the most effective as the smoke and ash contamination that gave it its colour also boosted its cleaning power.

SALTY LANGUAGE

It is from the Bible that we get the term 'salt of the earth' and knocking over salt is very bad luck: Judas Iscariot is knocking the salt over in the Leonardo Da Vinci painting *The Last Supper* and today if we knock salt over we throw it over our left shoulder. For years I did this without really considering why, but it is so that you can blind the devil lurking there.

De Pifcibus falfis, ficcatis, & fumigatis.

SALTING

Salt cod, salt herring and salt beef rivalled salt pig (bacon and ham) in the diet of most Tudor people.

Herring were gutted, opened out flat and laid in layers in barrels with a generous scattering of salt between each layer. The juices of the fish were naturally drawn out within the barrel and mingled with the salt to form brine. An individual fish treated in this way could become rather dried out, but a dozen fish packed tightly into a small watertight tub with coarse-grained sea salt is one of the easiest ways to preserve herring. They make a delicious meal eaten either raw straight from the tub, or fried with leeks and cream.

Cod, being a larger fish, whose flesh is thicker and less oily, required a different salting regime. After cleaning and filleting, the fish was rubbed on both sides with dry salt and hung up to air dry. As the moisture dripped out and the flesh dehydrated, bacterial activity was slowed and stopped, leaving the fish as hard as a board: it was able to remain edible, if kept dry, for up to a year.

❝ AS THE MOISTURE DRIPPED OUT AND THE FLESH DEHYDRATED, THE FISH WAS LEFT AS HARD AS A BOARD ❞

When you wished to eat it, you had to soak it for at least 24 hours in several changes of water, in order to both remove the salt and rehydrate the flesh. It's excellent poached in milk and served with boiled onions.

Salt beef used a mixture of both dry salt rubbing and barrel-packing to ensure a safe and successful preservation. First, the meat was cut into equal-sized pieces, so that each was preserved at the same rate. The account books of great houses and monasteries recorded how many pieces were regularly produced from each slaughtered animal. Documentary evidence from these and bones found at archaeological sites (in particular the sunken *Mary Rose* ship) indicated that it was usual to cut beef for salting into 2 lb pieces (including bone).

Each piece was firmly rubbed all over with a fine-grained salt and set aside to drain for a few hours. Meanwhile, brine was prepared, boiling up cheap grey salt in water, often with a bundle of herbs. The brine was allowed to completely cool, then the beef was stacked in it in a barrel for a period of around three days. The beef was then removed from the brine and stacked anew in a fresh barrel, packing around each piece with dry salt. The initial rubbing with salt, draining and three days in brine with complete change of salt, helped to remove a good deal of the meat juices and salt to penetrate to the centre of the joint, before the pieces were put into their final salt.

Barrels of salted fish and beef would keep all winter

Most of us these days only encounter salt beef in its Jewish American format – pastrami. I can however recommend a good boiled joint of salt beef, served with carrots, which is as hearty a meal today as it was back in Tudor times.

FISHPONDS

PETER

During the monastic period fishponds, along with deer parks, rabbit warrens and dovecotes were used as a way to provide fresh food throughout the year – as well as a source of income. However, due to the water engineering skills, the available land and the water management system that were needed, fishponds were generally associated with high status buildings and estates.

Remains of an abbey, reflected in fishpond

The earliest known fishponds in this country are Romano-British and date from the first century AD. They were stone-lined affairs and it is unclear how they were managed. Monastic fishponds appear to be just dug into the ground and therefore usually appear on clay. Up until the 1970s, very little archaeological investigation had been done into fishponds associated with monastic sites and it is only recently that they have really started to be studied.

The first records of monastic fishponds are from the 12th century, coinciding with the establishment and increase of the majority of monastic communities. The ponds themselves will often be associated with, or double up as, moats and mill ponds. Ponds were associated with wealthier monasteries, but the number of ponds was not an indication of status. Some sites have two to three ponds whereas others may have had up to twelve. If a site was near the sea or a large river, then there was less of a need for fishponds as there was already a supply of fish. As fishponds are generally on meadowland, sometimes their

❝ PONDS WERE ASSOCIATED WITH WEALTHIER MONASTERIES ❞

location was at a monastic grange – a farm that services the community but which may be run entirely by lay folk.

In order to feed the fish naturally, a fresh supply of water is needed to flush the pond. Usually there were leats that joined the ponds up and sluice gates that controlled the flow of water. There were rarely buildings associated with the fishponds and the only remaining monastic fish building in England is Meare Fish House. This was used as a facility to dry and salt the fish as well as offering accommodation for the water bailiff (Meare is a manor farmhouse associated with the powerful Glastonbury Abbey).

The ponds were managed by the systematic draining and sorting of the fish population. The silt in the bottom of the ponds was often dug out and used as a fertiliser but equally, there is evidence of ridge and furrow ploughing at the bottom of the ponds. This suggests that a possible catch-crop (a quick growing plant) was sowed and harvested before the pond was refilled and restocked. However, this could also be an indication that the pond was farmed after it fell out of use.

duo elementa tenet natura mediante
corpis i celi t ignis: t opa s tre v
eueniunt qz utriqz lenis t obsauun

RUSTLING

Security was a problem and ponds were often subject to fish rustling. This is perhaps why the ponds tend to be associated with the inner monastery estate. along with the gardens, the infirmary and the almonry (where alms for the poor were kept and distributed).

FISH STOCKS

During Lent it is thought that monks probably ate salted sea fish as it was a time of penance; fresh fish was a luxury item so it is more likely that the fish from the monastic fishponds was consumed on feast days. Also, the fish were a good source of food for the monastery when the monks abstained from meat on a Friday.

Prior to AD 1350 the fish that were initially farmed at monastery sites were mainly bream and pike. These fish have a five-year growth cycle, meaning that the ponds were drained once every five years for cleaning and repairs. When the ponds were empty, they are often recorded like any other pasture and it is indicated that they are left fallow.

During the latter half of the 14th century and the early 15th century, carp was introduced to fish farming and took off in a big way. The introduction coincided with economic change in the country, and a change in how the fishponds are managed. There was an increasing market for fresh fish in a society less and less concerned with religious restrictions on diet, and so the carp was an attractive fish. It is hardy enough to survive bad weather conditions such as a harsh winter and it can be transported easily. It also grows a lot faster which makes supplementary feeding of fish a lot more effective and reduces the monastic fish cycle to a period of three years.

TUDOR RECIPES

RUTH **I** have become a big fan of Tudor food. It's delicious, hearty and interesting. Not all of the dishes look terribly pretty, but they taste great. Most are fairly simple to make, relying – rather like good Italian cooking – upon the freshness and quality of the ingredients to shine through, rather than upon elaborate preparation.

Below are four fairly representative recipes, all of which I would recommend.

FRUMENTY
1 lb wholewheat grains
Water to boil
Two pints of milk, or a mixture of half milk and half single cream
Six egg yolks

This is a simple dish to make, somewhere between porridge and risotto. The recipe is for a sweet version, but there were also savoury frumenties with broth instead of milk and plenty of fresh herbs stirred in. Whilst frumenty appears in recipe books for use by the upper and middle classes and also in the menu lists of monasteries, it was in origin a very humble dish. Made with water and herbs, it also saved on miller's fees, providing hot filling food. In the highlands of Scotland, Wales and in the higher ground of the North of England, oats were the only reliable grain crop and frumenty and porridge are one and the same. In easier agricultural climes, the frumenty could be made of barley or wheat.

Boil the wheat in plain water until the grains burst, then drain and return to the pan with the milk. Simmer until the milk is mostly absorbed by the grain; at this

The finished Frumenty

If you have them, alexanders are a nice alternative to parsley in the fried beans recipe

point, take the pan off the heat and allow to cool for a minute or two. Beat the egg yolks together and stir them into the wheat and milk, allowing the residual heat to thicken the frumenty (much as you would if making real custard). Serve with a scattering of edible flowers dusting the top or a small handful of raisins.

TO FRYE BEANS

4 oz dried beans (originally a small field bean, you can use cannellini, borlotti or haricot beans)
Two large onions
Two large handfuls of parsley
4 oz butter

This is another simple dish that crossed class boundaries, and it is one of my favourites. It is a recipe for four very hearty portions, which can be served with a small portion of meat, perhaps a couple of rashers of bacon, or a fillet of white fish, for a complete meal. If you wished to use the bean dish simply as a side dish alongside potatoes, then you could halve the quantities.

Soak your beans overnight. Drain off the water and put them in a pan with fresh water, bring to the boil and simmer for an hour (if you buy tinned beans you can skip this stage, you will need three tins for this recipe). Drain the beans and put them to one side. Chop the onions and fry them in half of the butter until they begin to brown, then add the beans and the rest of the butter and stir it around for two minutes. Add the parsley, chopped, to the pot giving another couple of stirs. Serve.

OYSTERS IN BRUET

Two dozen Colchester oysters
1 oz breadcrumbs
Large splash of ale
Large splash of stock (beef stock is surprisingly nice,
    but fish stock is also good)
Pepper
Salt
Two blades of saffron

This recipe, from the abbot's table, calls for expensively acquired fresh oysters, packed alive in damp rushes and transported inland by cart or pack horse.

Take the oysters out of their shells and drop into simmering water for two minutes, then drain and lay upon a warm serving dish. In a small pan, bring the ale, stock, salt, pepper and saffron to a simmer and stir in the breadcrumbs to produce a thick sauce. Pour over the oysters and allow to stand for three or four minutes before serving.

POMMADORE

2 lb of beef mince
A dozen eggs
Pepper
Saffron
1 oz of raisins and currants

This is another recipe from the abbot's table, one for 'flesh days'. It was not however beyond the reach of prosperous farming people, at least on high days and holidays, if you were sparing with the pepper and raisins.

Grind the raisins and currants to a paste along with the pepper. Separate the eggs and add all of the whites to the raisins, mixing thoroughly. Now add in the minced beef: you will find it easiest to combine the beef and egg/raisin mixture if you work it with your hands. Meanwhile, put a large pan of water on to boil. Take a cloth, wet it and wring it out. Spread it out and sprinkle a little flour over the damp cloth, spreading it evenly. Place the Pommadore mixture in the centre of the cloth, forming an even cylinder that is twice as long as it is wide. Wrap the cloth around the mixture and tie the cloth at both ends – it will resemble a Christmas cracker. This cloth-wrapped package must be dropped into the boiling water and kept at a vigorous boil for 20 minutes.

Drain and unwrap the meat. If you are lucky enough to have access to a fireplace, spit and spit dogs, you can now put your parboiled Pommadore upon the spit and set it in front of the fire. If not, you may like to continue the cooking upon a barbecue, but it is also possible to use a conventional oven (place the meat upon a wire stand within your roasting tray so that the fat can drop free). Mix up the egg yolks with the saffron and paint a layer onto the Pommadore with a pastry brush.

Allow the meat to cook for three or four minutes, turning it several times, and ensure that the egg layer has set before adding another egg layer. Continue in this fashion, building up layers of golden yellow egg around the frequently turned meat. It should take around 15 minutes of turning and painting to use up all of the egg and finish the cooking through of the meat.

Serve either hot or cold.

Cooking over an open fire adds another dimension to the flavour as different woods can impart different smokey tastes to dishes such as pommadore

TUDOR
LIFE

The influences on Tudor pastimes came from the two great institutions of the age: the king and his parliament, and the Church. Activities could be banned by the parliament if they were not warlike enough, or banned by the Church for being immoral. So as much as entertainment and leisure were enjoyed, they were only filtered down throughout Tudor society under extremely controlled conditions.

The Tudors used their surroundings to create entertainment, though their social rank also dictated what kind of leisure was open to them. Sports like hunting and jousting were closed off to all but the aristocracy, but archery, by contrast, was a sport that transcended any social divides, such was its importance to the English military machine. Closer to home, Tudor communities handed down games and sports through generations, as ways to pass the time – on those rare occasions that there was no work to be done.

LEISURE AND ENTERTAINMENT

RUTH

Tudor life was not formally divided into work time and leisure time, but that does not mean that people were not able to find time for fun. There were always animals to be fed and mucked out, meals to be prepared and harvest to be brought in. But there were also slack times when work could be pushed onto the back burner, when the weeding could wait, the livestock could be left in the pasture and everyone could make do with bread, ale and cheese for dinner. Sunday afternoons were regarded as a good time for games, sport, chat and play when the agricultural calendar allowed.

Chatting and drinking with friends and neighbours formed a major part of leisure life

Meeting and chatting with friends formed a major part of Tudor leisure life. The more portable elements of work were often brought out into the street, so that work and friendship could go hand in hand. People popped around to friends' houses or met at the local alehouse. Youngsters gathered at the market cross to hang out together (to the occasional recorded grumbles of their elders). On a larger scale, the church organised fundraising 'ales' where everyone was invited to gather, drink the communally produced ale, socialise with the neighbours and dance.

DANCE

Fifteen years ago, an English manuscript dated to between 1480 and 1500 came to light. The manuscript gave the music and patterns of a group of dances: there are almost 50 tunes and 13 of them have dance patterns – but not steps – associated with them. A further group of dance patterns are also included but not linked to specific tunes.

" PEOPLE WERE DOING A LOT OF DANCING: AT CHURCH, ON THE VILLAGE GREEN, AT PUBS AND INNS, AT PEOPLE'S HOUSES "

The manuscript gives a real insight into the sort of dance that was going on in England, at least among the elite, at the time. We certainly know that people were doing a lot of dancing: records tell us of dancing at church, on the village green, at pubs and inns, at people's houses, at weddings and at Christmas celebrations. They tell us that the rich danced at court, that apprentices danced in the streets, groups of young women danced up on the hills and that mayors and aldermen held dances in civic buildings. We have no idea if they all danced the same dances to the same tunes, but we do know that people considered it to be fun and social.

The following is a description of a dance called 'Bugill'. You can see immediately some of the difficulties faced by historians of dance when they try to turn the evidence into an actual performance. There are plenty of clues, however, if you are a country or barn dancer and if you compare these instructions with those from slightly different times and places:

'*After the end of the trace evry man togeder two doublis then the first and the last forthright the medill contrary hym and torne face to face met in to a triangle wyse. Then all togeder ix singles compass. Then the last man throth whill the oder two conter hym. Then all ronde ix singles then all come togeder and depart with a torn theder thay come from. Then evry man from oder retrett iii. Then torn all at onys than all torn at onys trett and retrett then the medill torn the first aboute and leve hym on his left hand whill the last torne on his own place.*'

Music was alive, well and vigorous at court, in church and amongst ordinary folk

❝ WORK AND FRIENDSHIP COULD GO HAND IN HAND ❞

It seems to be a dance for three people stood in a line, beginning by facing the same way. All the dancers are referred to as men, but this was probably just the author's word for person as today the word 'mankind' stands in for the whole human race. Doubles and singles are steps that many modern folk dancers will recognise, as well as dance historians: a single is one step and then bring the feet together; a double is three steps before bringing the feet together and takes twice as long.

You can dance them in a number of different styles, walking or springing, with or without a hop, or something close to skipping – it's a matter of taste and conjecture which one our dancing master meant. 'Trett and

" CRUDELY SCRATCHED BOARDS
TO PLAY ALL OF THESE GAMES
SOMETIMES TURN UP BEHIND
CHOIR STALLS IN CHURCHES
WHERE BORED CHORISTERS
IDLED AWAY THEIR TIME "

retrett', meanwhile, translate roughly as go forwards and back. So the dancers move from forming a line into a triangle formation, then dance in a circle, then reverse the triangle, circle, and reverse the triangle.

GAMES

The first game to get its own dedicated printed book in English was chess, when William Caxton translated an older book from its original Latin and French handwritten incarnations. There were plenty of other board games about though. Backgammon, known as tables, was popular as were 'merels' (or Nine Men's Morris) and draughts. Crudely scratched boards to play all of these games sometimes turn up behind choir stalls in churches where bored choristers idled away their time.

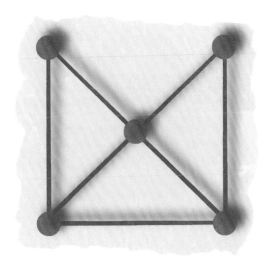

Boards were scratched upon furniture

Another simpler game involved two players, each with two counters and a board formed by five spots and some lines connecting them. To play you must first draw out four spots in a square and put the fifth right in the middle. Next, connect the four outside spots on three sides of the square by drawing three lines, leaving one side of the square open. Now connect all four outer spots to the central spot with a line.

The object of the game is to slide your counters along the lines to a position that traps your opponent, allowing them nowhere to move to. The first player sets a counter down on one of the spots, then the second does likewise. The first player sets down a second counter and so does the other player. At this point, four of the five spots are covered and there are limited options for movement. Each player moves in turn, trying to keep their own options open whilst boxing their opponent into a corner.

Skittles, or kayles as they were more commonly called, were found both in grand houses and at village alehouses: an original Elizabethan set survives in Cornwall at Trerice (managed by the National Trust). They appear frequently in court cases concerning drunken behaviour or disruption of church services. This wasn't because skittles had a particularly bad reputation, but because it

Skittles or 'kayles' was popular, especially at ale houses

was so common a game, played by both children and adults up and down the country at fairs and weddings, at church moneymaking social events and on late summer evenings when work was done.

A Sunday afternoon at the archery butts fulfilled a statutory obligation for men between 6 and 60 to practise with their bows once a week, but it also provided a social experience. Parties of friends went 'roving': they would choose a mark, perhaps a tree or particular clump of grass, then everyone would let loose a single arrow at the target to see who could come closest. A new mark was chosen and off they went again. It was played much as a modern game of friendly golf is played. Marks were chosen to test the players' ability: some near, some far, some at ground level, some at a tricky angle, some close to an arrow-losing hazard.

ROVING HAZARDS

One party of archery rovers in Sussex foolishly chose the shutters of a neighbouring inn as a mark and let loose their arrows, only to watch in horror as someone opened the shutters at that very moment and was pierced through the breast. (The resultant case at the coroner's court recorded a verdict of accidental death and no further action was taken.)

SPORT

Sport to most early Tudors often encompassed blood sports of one form or another. Bull and bear baiting were popular spectacles at which a good deal of money changed hands in bets. Cockfighting was cheaper to run and therefore more common, especially out in the countryside. Iron and steel spurs were attached to the legs of feisty birds, often reared and specially fed for the purpose. Forced into close proximity, the cocks followed their natural instincts, fighting for territory and access to the hens.

After hunting and hawking, tennis was the favoured sport of the aristocracy. It was a game that resembled modern squash more closely than modern lawn tennis. It was played within a walled court with a net and the ball was permitted to bounce off any of those walls. The game was played with rackets and a small dense ball similar to that now used by cricketers.

The young Prince Henry, second son to the King (destined, after the untimely death of his elder brother, to inherit his father's throne), was a very keen player of tennis. He had special tennis shoes and tennis doublets to play in, as well as access to several courts at different royal palaces. The rest of society did not have purpose built courts to play tennis, but a host of similar games up against the walls of churches, either with a racket, or more commonly using the hand to hit the ball, flourished in both Scotland and England.

Out in the towns and villages 'closh' and 'camping' were much more popular. Closh involved a wooden, long-handled club, wooden balls and hoops set in the ground in a form of croquet. Camping was a word used to describe free-form hockey and football. In some cases 'campers' are described as running around and kicking the ball; in others a stick is involved. Rules probably varied locally, from one group of players to another, perhaps even from one game to another amongst the same people.

The huge turnouts of traditional inter-community matches have attracted the attention of contemporary commentators and historians alike, complete with tales of hundreds per side and a range of tactics that included hiding the ball under women's skirts and swimming the river with it in games that ran from the spire of one church to that of another. However, most football – or camping – matches were small, informal kickabouts.

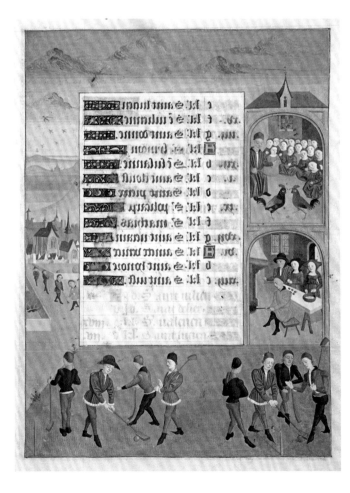

A game of closh

PILGRIMAGES

Pilgrimages were essentially a holiday from daily life, albeit a devotional one. A pilgrimage was seen as entering into a monastic way of life and leaving your worldly concerns behind. People going on pilgrimage would receive a blessing prior to embarking on their journey and they would often wear a long coarse garment signifying penance and carry a staff and a small purse.

A simple rosary to count off prayers

Reliquaries were built by craftsmen such as goldsmiths and monasteries made provision for pilgrims stopping on the way by providing food and lodgings. Due to the sheer number of

> **" DUE TO THE SHEER NUMBER OF PILGRIMS VISITING RELIGIOUS HOUSES TO VIEW THEIR RELICS, MANY MONASTERIES HAD TO MAKE ALTERATIONS "**

pilgrims visiting religious houses to view their relics, many monasteries had to make alterations. Several built interior passages known as ambulatories where pilgrims could walk and view a shrine or a reliquary without disturbing the monks as they went about their daily lives.

The original pilgrimages saw travellers heading either to Rome or the Holy Land. They began in the 4th century, when the Roman emperor Constantine converted to Christianity. Constantine's conversion made the practice of Christianity acceptable: he co-authored the Edict of Milan with the emperor Licinius which granted religious tolerance and meant property that had been confiscated from Christians was returned. At the time, the Romans still

controlled an empire of around 1.5 million square miles, centred around the Mediterranean (Constantine moved the capital from Rome to Constantinople). This meant travel was relatively easy and coupled with the new-found tolerance for Christianity, this made pilgrimages possible.

Constantine's most famous construction and perhaps one of the most sacred of all pilgrimage sites is the Church of the Holy Sepulchre. This is the church built on the site that is thought to be Golgotha (or Calvary) where Jesus was crucified. It incorporates a rock cut chamber thought to be the tomb of Joseph of Arimathea where Jesus was buried. Constantine also built a basilica dedicated to St Peter in Rome.

For many years, the Holy Land and the more easily accessible Rome were the focus of pilgrimages: either through their location or through relics, they were connected directly with the life of

Christ leading a pilgrimage to Santiago

Jesus, the apostles (in Rome's case Peter) and the disciples (in Rome's case Paul). However, during the Middle Ages relics of significance began to spread and the focus of pilgrimages began to change. It was now possible to visit relics and make a pilgrimage without leaving England at all.

> ❝ IT WAS NOW POSSIBLE TO VISIT RELICS AND MAKE A PILGRIMAGE WITHOUT LEAVING ENGLAND AT ALL ❞

Above: Pilgrims on the road to Canterbury
Opposite: Canterbury Cathedral

Pilgrimages still go on today. If you visit any religious site that attracts visitors or pilgrims, there is always a thriving trade in food, accommodation and souvenirs – and it would have been no different during the Tudor period: the George Hotel and Pilgrims Inn built in Glastonbury in the 15th century are two such examples that continue to thrive on the pilgrimage trail.

A PILGRIM'S TALE
Pilgrimages inspired many works of art including Chaucer's *Canterbury Tales*. The premise for the tales is that a group of pilgrims from a number of different social backgrounds are embarking on a pilgrimage from Southwark in London to the popular pilgrimage site of Canterbury. In order to win a free meal they are engaged in a story-writing contest.

ARCHERY

If you had to choose a national sport for modern England, then it would probably be football. If you were feeling argumentative, you might suggest rugby or cricket were just as important, possibly based on social divisions. But in the Middle Ages through to Tudor times the English practised a martial art: longbow archery.

Derek, our bowyer, takes aim with his war bow – the yeoman warrior's weapon of choice

It might seem strange in the 21st century to think that after church on a Sunday men would train to kill, but such was the nature of Tudor England that the skill to attack and defend was still incredibly important. England had been through the Crusades, wars with their Celtic neighbours and France, not to mention internal conflicts. As such, it is no surprise that the country's pastime of choice was also a test of skill at arms. Archery, as well as a social activity to be enjoyed by friends and family, was a discipline of strength and skill that could one day be employed on the battlefield.

> **" IT IS NO SURPRISE THAT THE COUNTRY'S PASTIME OF CHOICE WAS ALSO A TEST OF SKILL AT ARMS "**

Peter demonstrates his ability to 'loose' an arrow.
One certainly does not 'fire' an arrow!

BOWS AND ARROWS

The bow and arrow is one of those inventions that archaeologists believe happened independently in various parts of the world. Quite simply it is a stout bendy stick and a string and when pulled taut and released fires a smaller pointy stick. Longbows are relatively easy to make which means they can be produced quickly, though this also meant that during Tudor times there was a huge demand for appropriate wood, with merchants often bringing in staves as ballast.

The heart and sap wood of hazel

The longbow has a D-shaped cross-section, made from the sapwood and the heartwood of the yew tree, although boxwood was also used. The sap and heartwoods are good under tension and compression giving the bow its flexibility, strength and power. At around six feet long the bow has an estimated draw weight of 110–130 lbs (although estimates vary).

FIRING A BOW

It is said that the skeletons of archers can be identified by their deformities. Having regularly shot a bow and arrow, my arm, back and chest strength are imbalanced based on how I draw my bow. However, the way that the modern bow is drawn is different to how the longbow was. The modern bow has a lower draw weight, so you can start with the bow extended in one arm and draw the string with the other. The longbow, on the other hand, requires you to bodily step into the bow, which means that you essentially draw it like a chest expander.

Tom drawing his bow while concentrating on the target

The bow is tipped at both ends with cow horn and is strung with either flax, hemp or linen string. Strings are usually waxed with beeswax to help protect them, but that is where the bow technology stops. There are no sights, so more than physically building yourself up I think practice was to ensure that when you came to load, draw and fire the bow you weren't thinking about the action, but it was just muscle memory: you could see your target and knew how to hit it. The longbow is deathly accurate, especially over a short range.

An arrow nocked on the string

In order to fire a bow, you also needed clothing protection. On the arm that holds the bow you wear what is known as a bracer. This is a leather shield that stops the string from hitting the flesh of your forearm. I once forgot to put my bracer on – never again! You also need to wear a tab. This is a small piece of leather with two or three holes for your fingers and it acts as a barrier between the string and your hand. If you don't wear one, the string cuts into your fingers. This may not be a problem in the short term, but it would become very painful, if not debilitating, in the long term.

THE ARROW

When people talk about archery, they almost always focus on the bow. However, it is the arrows that eventually do the killing. When firing an arrow from a bow, you are faced with a problem known as the 'archer's

The flights and nock of an arrow

The weight of an arrowhead meant that power was sustained throughout flight

paradox': the bowstring is strung between two points and when released will propel its force in a straight line to the middle of the wood. The arrow can't pass through this wood so instead has to curve around it.

Arrows are made of a stiff wood such as birch (arrows found on the *Mary Rose* were made mainly of poplar but also ash, beech and hazel). The stiffness of the arrow is known as the spine and the stiffer an arrow, the more spine it has. When a bowstring is released, the shock of power – the transference of the potential energy stored in the bow to the kinetic energy given to the arrow – causes the arrow to physically deform. This means that the arrow can flex around the bow a bit like a salmon leaping up a stream. However, this also means that the archer needs to pair a bow with certain arrows. The more powerful the bow, the more spine the arrow needs.

BATTLE ARROWS
Victories with the longbow aren't necessarily about how many arrows you fire but exactly when and where you fire them. Any arrows you have fired will lodge in the ground and can be picked up by an advancing army who needs ammunition. This is why slightly longer arrows known as flight arrows were sometimes deployed in battle. They had a longer range than standard arrows and could be fired in the hopes of tricking the enemy into thinking that they were within bow range and firing off a volley of their main arrows.

" THOSE THAT WEREN'T KILLED WOULD HAVE THEIR WOUNDS INFECTED BY THE DIRT "

An arrow has four main parts: a head, a shaft, flights and a nock. The nock is the groove at the end that the string sits in. The flights are the three or more feather sections that stabilise the arrow as it moves through the air; the head is what does the damage. It is thought that because archers kept their arrows in the ground in front of them, when they were fired and hit their targets, those that weren't killed would have their wounds infected by the dirt. However, if the arrow did hit you, the dirt was probably the least of your worries. The arrow heads used in war were generally broad heads designed to rip a wound that would be hard to heal and cause a large amount of bleeding. The barb was designed so that the easiest and cleanest way to get the arrow out was to push it all the way through.

Derek teaching Peter the ins and outs of longbows

THE LONGBOW IN BATTLE

One cannot underestimate the effect the longbow had on English, and consequently, world history. It was quite literally a game-changer. By harnessing the skill and strength of the English and Welsh yeomanry, the English kings were able to take small, mobile armies to France and take on the immense might of their chivalric armies. The longbow men formed a vital part of invading armies, respected by the kings that led them and feared by the enemies they faced. Perhaps the greatest of battles fought between the kingdoms of England and France were the battles of Crécy (1346), Poitiers (1356) and Agincourt (1415) during the Hundred Years War. French numbers, French armour, French horses and French courage could not compete against well-disciplined English soldiers, armed predominantly with the longbow.

The benefits of the longbow lay in range, rapidity of fire and the destructive effect of a hailstorm of arrows on massed ranks of men and horses. The range of a longbow is estimated at any distance between 200 and 300 yards. Though its effectiveness against plate armour at 300 yards was limited, at anything between 50 and 150 yards, the longbow was destructive. Using the

The longbow in use at the Battle of Agincourt

longbow as a close-combat weapon was first used against the English by the Welsh to great effect, but in the best traditions of all conquering armies the English took what worked and utilised those tactics themselves in future conflicts.

Five thousand archers could put enough metal-tipped arrows in the air to create killing zones hardly seen again until the invention of the machine gun. Over ten arrows a minute could be fired by skilled bowmen, compared to four to five musket balls by the highly-trained British Redcoat during the Napoleonic Wars. This massively increased the chances of hitting their targets: even if not every arrow that landed was a kill shot, the injuries and the havoc caused in the massed ranks of attacking men meant that the enemy were often nullified as an effective force before they got close enough to cause any serious damage. Injuries to horses and the less protected parts of humans such as arms and legs disrupted the enemy's plans and had a deadening effect on their morale.

Coupled with the fact that the longbow could be used anywhere, in all conditions, meant that the enemy were never safe. With proper care and attention the longbow was an all-weather weapon, allowing it an extended lifespan even after the introduction of gunpowder. This meant that the transition from wood and hemp to firepower was gradual not quick. The Battle of Agincourt in October 1415 might be considered the zenith of the longbow's effectiveness, but it would be a long time before it would fall from favour.

THE FALL OF THE LONGBOW

The downside of the longbow revolved around the raw power required to use it efficiently. Longbow training began in childhood so that the strength required for using a war bow in battle was already developed by manhood, but this manpower pool was always at threat from disease, starvation and attrition through war. These concerns meant that England needed to ensure it had a constant supply of healthy, strong men capable of using a longbow in order to wage war in France.

> " LONGBOW TRAINING BEGAN IN CHILDHOOD SO THAT THE STRENGTH REQUIRED FOR USING A WAR BOW IN BATTLE WAS ALREADY DEVELOPED BY MANHOOD "

This was a constant cause of worry to the English Parliament and as early as 1487, an act was passed curtailing the price of longbows so that they were accessible to all (crossbows, by contrast, could only be used by wealthier landowners). Henry VIII himself was a keen archer and in 1513 a worried English Parliament, once again fearing the loss of longbow skills, wrote into law that every household should contain a longbow and four arrows, and any man over 17 and under 60 was required to practise after church on a Sunday.

Even so, the longbow's days were numbered. The rise of the crossbow, with its ease of use, meant that anybody could fire one and the increasing effectiveness of gunpowder weapons such as the arquebus spelled the end of the longbow as a viable weapon. At the same time, the growth of other sports and pursuits such as skittles, tennis and bowls, all of which were less physically demanding, meant the inclination was no longer there to train frequently.

A CLASS OF THEIR OWN

The archer was not considered a member of the peasantry in England, as the French considered them, but almost became their own class. Archers were men with skilled jobs and professions who could also use the bow; English kings and knights recognised this difference, a stark contrast to the coerced French peasantry fighting under the French kings. Yeoman farmers were exactly the kind of men to train with the longbow because they ate a decent diet and their work was so physical, pushing their bodies in their everyday life and thus maintaining the conditioning required for using the bow.

After our training, we put our skills to the test in an archery contest

Arguably the longbow's last great battle came in 1513 against the Scots at the Battle of Flodden, but by the end of the Tudor period the usage of the longbow was falling. English military commanders in the later 16th century still considered the longbow a viable weapon but as tactics and weaponry changed on the continent, England was soon to follow. Even so, it is worth noting that during the Napoleonic Wars, the Duke of Wellington was still keen to form a company of longbow men for stealth and range purposes. The gun might have dominated warfare from the 17th century onwards but the longbow should always be remembered as a weapon that allowed England to compete with the big nations of Europe.

> " DURING THE NAPOLEONIC WARS, THE DUKE OF WELLINGTON WAS STILL KEEN TO FORM A COMPANY OF LONGBOW MEN FOR STEALTH AND RANGE PURPOSES "

The longbow's greatest legacy was the destruction of the chivalric code, changing the idea of warfare being up close and personal: death at a distance was now the future. Its long history has ensured a strong place in the English psyche and even today, there are a wide range of clubs and societies dedicated to its practice.

THE FUTURE: LIFE BEYOND THE FARM

PETER

hen Henry VIII came to the throne in 1509, it is estimated that the Church owned and controlled between one fifth and one third of all of the landed wealth in England. The Church answered to the Pope and, at the time, so did the King. Yet within just over 30 years, this status quo that had existed for centuries would be turned upside-down, and the Tudor period would become known throughout history as one of the most significant turning points in England's history.

Henry VIII, who successfully wiped out monasteries in just under two decades

THE ENGLISH REFORMATION

Pope Leo X bestowed the title Fidei Defensor (Defender of the Faith) on Henry after he wrote the pamphlet *Asserto Septem Sacramentorum* in 1521, defending the seven sacraments (including marriage) and swearing allegiance to the Vatican. This was a treatise speaking out against the idea of the Protestant Reformation that had been initiated in continental Europe by the German monk Martin Luther (1483–1546), who publicised the Ninety-Five Theses on the Power and Efficacy of Indulgences. It defended the status quo against Luther's claims of corruption and the abuse of the Church's position in society with the granting of indulgences: rather than paying a penance for sin it was possible to do a good deed to absolve yourself and with a sufficient donation you could 'buy your way into heaven'.

> ❝ RATHER THAN PAYING A PENANCE FOR SIN IT WAS POSSIBLE TO DO A GOOD DEED TO ABSOLVE YOURSELF AND WITH A SUFFICIENT DONATION YOU COULD 'BUY YOUR WAY INTO HEAVEN' ❞

In 1527, however, Henry asked the Pope for a divorce from his first wife Catherine of Aragon. The request was denied. Five years later in 1532, Thomas Cromwell drafted the Ecclesiastical Appeals Act that stopped all appeals to Rome and made the monarch the final resting place for all legal matters. The following year, Henry married Anne Boleyn while still married to Catherine, an act that led to him being excommunicated from the Church. Although it is believed that Henry maintained his faith and considered himself a Catholic for the rest of his life, the following year the Act of Supremacy was passed, confirming Henry VIII as the Supreme Governor of all churches in England and effectively severing the Church of England from the Catholic Church. This was bad news for the monasteries, and everyone associated with them.

> ❝ THIS WAS BAD NEWS FOR THE MONASTERIES, AND EVERYONE ASSOCIATED WITH THEM ❞

THE DISSOLUTION OF THE MONASTERIES

Monasteries were not only landowners, they were also centres of crafts, industries and effectively a source of materials. It is far easier to strip lead out of ornate windows than it is to mine it and smelt it from the ground. Furthermore, if as king you are fighting costly wars with Scotland and France, then the monasteries offered an easy source of cash. Thomas Cromwell started inventorying the assets of the Church, and this led to him or his commissioners visiting all the monasteries, friaries, nunneries, convents and priories. Soon after this, the first Act of Suppression was passed. This enabled Cromwell to dissolve all the smaller religious houses in England that had an annual income of less than £200.

The Protestant Reformation that had taken place on the continent was primarily born out of religious ideals. The English reformation was very much a political affair and when the dissolution of the monasteries began, it was

> ❝ WHEN THE DISSOLUTION OF THE MONASTERIES BEGAN, IT WAS MET WITH A CERTAIN AMOUNT OF RESISTANCE ❞

met with a certain amount of resistance. The first uprising was in Lincoln and was focused not against the King but against the act of dissolution itself. Thousands of protesters marched on and occupied Lincoln Cathedral; they were soon dispersed when Henry sent Charles Brandon whom he had appointed the Duke of Suffolk. The leaders of the uprising were eventually captured and taken to the village of Tyburn for execution on the Tyburn Tree (a three legged gallows that enabled multiple executions and stood very near to the site of Marble Arch in London).

Thomas Cromwell,
as painted by Hans
Holbein the Younger,
whom he patronised

" THE DISSOLUTION OF THE MONASTERIES AFFECTED OVER 800 RELIGIOUS COMMUNITIES "

The dissolution of the monasteries seems to have started out as genuine monastic reform, with the intention of thinning out hangers-on and a tightening up of religious vows. Monks and nuns were given the option to leave with pensions or move to larger religious houses. However, as the saying goes, the road to hell is paved with good intentions, and soon it became clear that the total abolition of religious orders was on the horizon. A second Act of Suppression was passed in 1539, enabling Cromwell to target the remaining larger religious houses and a year later in March of 1540 the dissolution of the monasteries was complete.

The dissolution of the monasteries affected over 800 religious communities. The result was that the rich got richer and the poor got poorer: the process could only be carried out by Henry promising the lands recovered to influential members of society and as a result, the sick, the old and the poor lost the charity they had received from the monasteries. Works of art and a wealth of documented knowledge in the monastic libraries were lost and building materials were stripped out for reuse elsewhere. It is amazing just how total the whole dissolution was in a period of less than 20 years.

CROMWELL'S END
Despite being rewarded for his role in the dissolution, Thomas Cromwell had also made many enemies at court. He suggested to Henry a union between him and Anne of Cleeves (who looked nothing like her picture). When Henry VIII urged him to find a legal solution to avoid a marriage, Thomas was unable to provide one. He stated that it would upset the Germans and the marriage went ahead, though never consummated. Thomas Cromwell was then executed without trial for high treason on 28th July 1540.

GLASTONBURY

Glastonbury Abbey was the most powerful monastery at the time of the dissolution. At the time the abbot, Blessed Richard Whiting, had ratified the first Act of Suppression and in doing so gained assurances that his abbey was safe from dissolution. In January 1539, he refused to surrender the abbey as events worsened for the monastic community. Later that year Whiting was sent to the Tower of London so he could be examined by Cromwell before being sent back to Somerset. After various 'trials', he was convicted of robbing Glastonbury church and he and two of his monks were tied to hurdles, dragged by horses to the top of Glastonbury Tor and hung, drawn and quartered.

Folklore suggests that the nursery rhyme 'Little Jack Horner' refers to Blessed Richard Whiting's steward Thomas Horner. Horner, it is said, was sent to London with a huge Christmas pie (presumably Christmas 1538) containing the deeds to a number of manorial properties. It is thought that Horner opened it up and removed the deeds to Mells Manor in Somerset, which included the rights to the lead mines in the Mendip hills; the Latin for lead is

Elizabeth I, the fifth and final monarch of the Tudor period

plumbum, hence the line about pulling out a plum. The rumour is denied.

AFTERMATH

In 1559, during the reign of Henry's younger daughter Elizabeth I, England officially became Protestant. For the next 232 years (bar a couple of years during the reign of James II) it was illegal to be a Catholic. In Ye Olde Tea Shoppe in Midhurst, there is a plaster wall painting dating from Elizabeth's reign depicting 1 Kings 21, with Ahab and Naboth in Tudor costume. It is thought to reflect the local Catholic feelings of being robbed of their religion.

> ❝ CATHOLICISM SURVIVED IN SECRET, WITH UNDERGROUND MASSES BEING HELD AND PRIESTS BEING HIDDEN FROM SOLDIERS DURING RAIDS ❞

Catholicism survived in secret, with underground masses being held and priests being hidden from soldiers during raids. One of the most famous houses built during the period and now owned by the Archdiocese of Birmingham is Harvington Hall. It has the greatest number of priest holes of any house in Britain, the most impressive being the one in the library discovered when a boy who was messing around fell through a wattle and daub panel. Harvington Hall was also one of the first houses to have corridors, so when a raid was under way soldiers would become confused about where they had been. The chapel is located at the very top of the house with panoramic views of the landscape. Even with intimate knowledge of the house and a good pair of trainers on it takes several minutes to get up there, so there was time to hide the altar goods and the priest.

After 1610, the executions of priests and people harbouring them tailed off and in 1791 Catholic worship became legal again. However, the majority of Catholic churches in England are now buildings that are not much older than 200 years. Although, this said, the rich fabric that was the monastic tradition is still evident around us and resonates in our lives today. We, as a society, and even as individuals, owe so much of our modus operandi to the monks, nuns and friars, as well as the craftspeople, the merchants and, of course, the farmers of that early Tudor period. God bless them all.

INDEX

PICTURE CREDITS